Climbing Out of Depression

Sue Atkinson

THE
PRISM
PROJECT

**The Prism Project
PO BOX 6031
Bishop's Stortford
Herts CM23 1PP**

If this book inspires you,
and you would like to read more self-help,
life enhancing, positive material,
please ask your Librarian for other Prism Project
donations, or contact us at the above address

Help us to help others
We welcome your comments or suggestions
and invite you to support us on your release.
Please take care of this book

For those who held onto the lifeline
when the going was tough,
for those who sat with me at the bottom of the cliff
and held my hand,
and for those who showed me, by their love,
that the climb was worthwhile

Copyright © 1993 Sue Atkinson

The author asserts the moral right
to be identified as the author of this work

Published by
Lion Publishing plc
Mayfield House, 256 Banbury Road
Oxford OX2 7DH, England
www.lion-publishing.co.uk
ISBN 0 7459 2248 1

First edition 1993
10 9

A catalogue record for this book is available
from the British Library

Printed and bound in Great Britain
by Cox & Wyman Ltd, Reading

Contents

Introduction   7

PART 1: ROCK-CLIMBING FOR LEMMINGS

Instant cures?   9

Why rock-climbing?   13

PART 2: HOW DID I GET HERE?

Sitting on the rocks at the foot of the cliff   16

Finding the cave: ideas for the very bad days   20

What is depression?   23

What causes depression?   27

Being kind to ourselves   34

PART 3: IS CLIMBING FOR ME?

Someone to talk to   38

The 'goodenough' principle   40

Strategies for living   42

What about professional therapy?   47

Preparing for the bad days   50

PART 4: FIRST STEPS

How can I get started?   58

What preparations can I make?   62

Things we need to take   69

Life is difficult   72

Things to leave behind   79
Negative thinking   84

PART 5: HANGING ON
Getting to know ourselves   96
Emotions are OK   99
Overcoming fear, worry and panic   103
Understanding our anger   108
Managing guilt   112
Understanding how we see ourselves:
our self-esteem   114
Boosting our self-esteem   116
Understanding the 'losses' in our lives   122
Understanding stresses   125
Fears   129

PART 6: FALLING OFF
Falling off   135

PART 7: MAKING PROGRESS
Picking ourselves up and having another go   140
Using our dreams to help us   146
Loneliness   149
Reaching the overhang and facing the impossible   153
'You'll be glad this happened'?   156
Missing the foothold   160
Reaching the top   164
Now for the mountain!   168
Resources   173

Introduction

Ways to use this book

◆ The book is written to be read in little bits. The concentration span of most people who are depressed is so limited that reading in small chunks is often all that is possible.

◆ Dip into the parts of the book that appeal to you today or most fit your mood.

◆ Skip what doesn't seem relevant to you today.

◆ Go back later to the parts that you don't understand or that make you angry.

◆ Each chapter is more or less self-contained, but I have sometimes referred to other relevant bits on the same theme at the end of the chapters. In this way you can use the book to follow up certain points that may seem particularly relevant to you.

◆ Try the activities. Don't just read them! The book is intended to spark off your own thinking.

◆ Ideas for other reading are given at the end (pages 174–75), along with addresses of some useful organizations.

◆ Using the book with a friend may help you to get more from it.

PART 1

ROCK-
CLIMBING
FOR
LEMMINGS

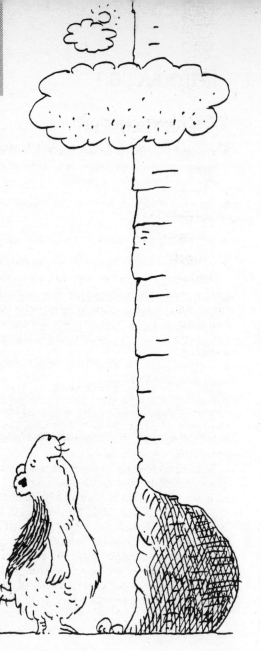

1

Instant cures?

This book is intended for people who feel

sad

lonely

despairing

depressed

suicidal.

It does not contain any miracle cure, instant healing, or health, wealth and happiness just over the page. Any book that offers such things, or any person who tells you a simple way to feel better ('count your blessings, dear', or 'eat more fresh fruit and vegetables') is to be regarded with the very deepest suspicion.

What this book isn't

This book isn't '10 Easy Steps out of Depression'. I have a horror of those books! They may well work for some people, but what if I do the steps and I'm just as depressed at the end of it all? I just know that would happen to me.

In my experiences of depression over several years, recovering is never simple, and certainly never easy. Those people who tell us it is easy and that we must pull our socks up are simply wrong!

This book is less of a 'how-to', and much more of a 'why', book. I think if we know 'why', we will be more in a position to take appropriate steps to know how to get out of it all.

It does have some 'how-to' suggestions. But they are only suggestions. They are based on things that I have done, or that others I know have done. Some of the activities have been suggested by people who work with those who are depressed.

My qualifications for writing the book

I have been depressed many times in my life, and I have talked with and lived alongside other depressed people during those years. And I survived!

I'm not writing it as an 'expert'. Nor am I writing it because I think I have found all the answers. It is a book about seeking out the right questions. Not all the book will help you. You may hate bits of it. Ignore these and go onto another section, but when you feel stronger, return to the bit you hated and ask yourself why you hated it. What was it that got to you?

The reality of depression

It is a very, very difficult thing to climb up out of depression. One day we seem to be near the top. The next we realize that we are actually down near the bottom again.

But we can do it! That is one of the Great Truths about depression—it doesn't last for ever.

For each of us the climb is slightly different. What works for me or my friend may not work for you. Or it may not work for you just yet. But as with any tool or aid for life's problems, what we get out of it is directly proportional to what we put in. You need to *do* the activities to get the most from the book.

> **I hear and I forget**
> **I see and I remember**
> **I do and I understand.**
>
> **Old Chinese proverb**

On days when depression is very bad, it may be best just to browse through some of the book, and return to the activities another day.

Getting better from depression is not a spectator sport

Getting better from depression is like rock-climbing. No one ever got up a climb by just thinking about it. We only get up with a great deal of blood, sweat and tears, a fair bit of courage, some falling off and starting again, and a large amount of determination.

Before you give up and decide that you have none of those qualities, it is important to see that even opening this book took some courage. For the depressed person, to do *anything* takes courage.

There will be no major solution to the suffering of humanity until we reach some understanding of who we are, what the purpose of creation was, what happens after death. Until those questions are resolved we are caught.

Woody Allen

I suggest that you need a notebook. It doesn't have to be a smart, thick hardback journal. It can be a cheap little jotter from the market. What is important is that it is something you feel happy with. It is yours and only yours. No one else reads it. So you need to find a place to keep it safe.

◆ Maybe writing fills you with horror! Don't worry. Write if it is helpful. If it isn't, just ignore those activities that are about writing.

◆ This 'journal', as I will call it, can be as important as you want it to be.

◆ If you are more of a talker than a writer, you might just want to jot down notes of what you want to discuss with someone.

◆ The important thing is that we externalize our ideas somehow.

For me it is writing. For some people it is talking, or painting, or cooking, or putting all their energies into an aggressive sport. If we do use a journal or notebook, one of its important functions is to help to get our thoughts and feelings outside of us. There are other ways that we can choose to externalize our feeling and thinking, such as

talking

cooking

gardening

drawing

painting

dancing.

11

By putting our feelings and thoughts outside ourselves in these ways, we can get clues as to what makes us depressed. For example, if, as we dig the garden, we are thinking repeatedly about how to get on with some member of our family, it is highly likely that this is getting us down far more than we may have realized.

If we try to get our thinking out where we can look at it, we will have some power over it. If we have some power over what we are thinking, it will not control us so much. We will be more in charge of our lives. This power over the direction of our lives is important in our recovery from depression.

My own journals over the years contain ideas, thoughts, moans, prayers, pencil sketches, and drafts of furious letters to people. When I was in hospital it also contained a calendar—I became so confused I couldn't work out even which season it was. Your journal may be very different and the suggested activities are just starting points. They are not a set of fixed things you must do.

I lay in bed staring at the darkness—hopeless. For weeks I had been unable to eat or sleep and was gripped with the fierceness of my neurosis. This time I knew I was not going to get better by myself.

Martha Maughon

12

2

Why rock-climbing?
The trouble with the rat race is that even if you win you're still a rat.

Lily Tomlin, actress

One of my favourite activities is rock-climbing. When I was six-
teen I discovered that when I was faced with an almost impossible
challenge, a bit of me got energized. I soon got hooked on the
unbelievably fantastic feeling of getting to the top. Later on,
after years of depression which went on into my twenties and
thirties, I took up climbing again. I began to see how like life
it is. It feels like hell while you are doing it, but getting to the
top gives the feeling that nothing will ever be so difficult again.

So I'm using rock-climbing as an illustration of the struggle
out of depression.

Why lemmings?

I identify with lemmings—little brown furry creatures of the
Scandinavian tundra. The lemming is often thought of as an animal that leaps off cliffs to commit suicide. When naturalists tell
us that this is not what they really do, we feel a bit cheated!

Apparently what lemmings really do is emigrate. In some
years—'lemming-years'—there are too many of them and food
is scarce. No one is really quite sure what it is that makes one of
these 'lemming-years', but litter after litter of baby lemmings
are born. Perhaps the weather is good, or there is plentiful food,
but whatever it is, lemmings go on and on having babies. Maybe
Mrs Lemming just feels broody. It could be changes in the
climate, or in their food sources. As yet, naturalists are not sure.

The outcome is that on the overcrowded slopes of the hillside
the instinct to spread out is activated. Hundreds of lemmings
scurry off as if their lives depended on it, in a great swathe or
whatever the collective noun for lemmings is—a 'courage' of
lemmings maybe—and if they happen to get to the cliff edge,
over they go.

13

It is this that has led to the belief that they commit suicide. What they are really doing is rushing off to find some island or patch of hillside where they can feed in peace, without having friends and relations gobbled up by bands of marauding goshawks. So it is all really done for the survival of the species, but given the height of some Norwegian fjord cliffs, it is hardly surprising that many of them perish in pursuit of this survival. Hence their acts of courage have been mistaken by mere humans as suicide.

Lemmings have been suspected of suicide for so long that it is hard to change the image. That goes for a lot of us. How we *were* is what we get stuck with.

Depressed people can identify with lemmings. We feel the urge to emigrate, or get away from all that haunts us, or wish that we could start life all over again. For many of us, life is so terrible that we can believe that death would be some sort of relief. Certainly it could be no worse.

So this book is written for:

◆ those who want to jump, or have jumped, 'over the cliff' (some feel they were pushed).

◆ those sitting at the bottom of the cliff.

◆ those who are so overwhelmed and confused that they have no idea where they are and how they got there. They certainly have no idea of what they might do about it—or even if they want to do anything about it because it is all so awful.

◆ those who, looking up at the cliff, really want to be back at the top again. But they feel they could do with a lot of help if they are ever going to attempt the climb.

We promise according to our hopes and perform according to our fears.

François Duc de la Rochefoucauld

PART 2

HOW DID I GET HERE?

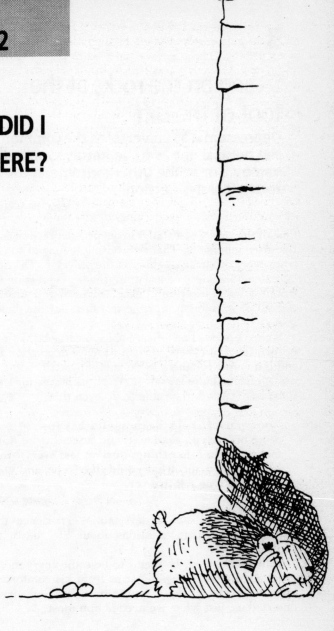

3

Sitting on the rocks at the foot of the cliff

Depression is as universal as the common cold. It can be so slight as to be hardly worth the name ... or at the other extreme, it can almost totally paralyse action.

Myra Chave-Jones

One of the very worst things in deepest depression and despair is the utter loneliness. That devastating feeling of total alienation from every other living thing in the universe. The intense mental pain and anxiety of isolation divides depression and despair from the much less painful experiences of difficulty and sadness that all of us suffer from time to time. But the dividing line is thin.

Some depressed people are able to carry on with a relatively normal life. For others, certain stages of depression are too dark and too empty for them to do anything at all. Some people can manage a few things for self-survival, such as eating and drinking, some have ceased to be able to do even that.

None of us can help the things life has done to us. They're done before you realize it, and once they're done they make you do other things until at last everything comes between you and what you'd like to be, and you have lost your true self forever.

Eugene O'Neil

Depression is such a devastating experience that we ask ourselves very basic questions about life, death and human exprience.

If there is a God, he seems to be some angry monster, some cruel alien who is laughing at us from his comfortable seat on high. So maybe we don't want him as our God anyway. He has deserted us, just when we needed him most.

I've tried appeasing this God. 'If you will just . . .' 'If you will take these feelings away, I'll love you for ever and do anything you want.' But it didn't work. I know I don't deserve to be loved. It was all my fault. I feel guilty. Ashamed. Hopeless. Useless. Stupid. A fraud.

People are laughing at me, and I feel so afraid. I know I'm no good. In the depths of the night, fear grips my heart. It paralyzes my mind.

But most of all, I feel very, very alone.

We're all in this together—by ourselves.

Lily Tomlin

It is the dark abyss of depression. The pit. The bell jar. Hell. The bottom of the steepest cliff at midnight. The tide is coming in and there is no escape.

How do I know if I am depressed?

It is possible not to realize that you are depressed. Ordinary times of sadness that we come to expect—we might call these 'the blues'—are very difficult to distinguish from mild depression. If we are experiencing depression for the first time we may well simply not know what is happening to us. Depression is talked about a little more in our society nowadays than it used to be, but it is still an area of mystery. This makes it very hard for us to deal with. We feel 'odd', out of step with others and rather mystified about what is going on. Much of this book is about why we are depressed. It is much easier to get out of depression if we understand it and can gradually come to see what it is all about.

The symptoms of depression

At first it may be no more than an insidious creeping sadness and lethargy. In mild depression that may be all we experience. But there are many different levels of depression—from this vague feeling of malaise to extreme symptoms such as hearing voices, hallucinations and the suicidal feelings which sometimes accompany the deepest depressions. The other symptoms are many and varied and include:

17

irritability

withdrawal

crying

anger

weight loss or gain

lack of concentration

violent mood swings

fear and anxiety

an over-awareness of criticisms

feelings of guilt

hopelessness

bursting into tears

feeling inadequate

a changed pattern of sleep—either waking up very early or an inability to get to sleep

no interest in food—or over-eating as a kind of comfort

uncontrollable feelings of total despair.

There seems no point in doing anything, and the things that used to motivate us, like cooking, or gardening, a favourite hobby, going to the cinema, sex, music or whatever, now fail to interest us. It is this change of lifestyle that is often the clearest indicator of depression. You may have few other symptoms, but inside yourself you know that something is wrong. That is depression.

What does it feel like?

At its worst, depression is like a thick cloud that comes down upon us totally unexpectedly. It is fear of the deepest darkness. It is like walking alone on the Yorkshire Moors at night. Like living on an alien planet. Like suddenly and unexpectedly becoming blind, deaf, dumb, paralyzed and penniless. But because you are none of these things the world expects you to cope.

But you can't. And no one can hear your cry. You can speak words but the world has no way to hear you. You are utterly terrified. You want to evaporate. You want out of life.

The mass of men lead lives of quiet desperation.
Henry Thoreau (1817–62)

A broken leg tells the world there is something wrong. But when your mind shuts off from reality in order to survive, you have no easy way to tell the world that you are hurting inside.

Images of depression

Feelings of darkness and of being imprisoned give rise to various pictures of depression. I've always thought of it as a very deep, narrow, straight-sided pit, or the bottom of a cleft in a cliff. It is totally dark and there are no footholds. Scrabbling up the edge is hopeless. I am alone and it is breathtakingly silent.

Others who are depressed see it as a prison, a steep hill, a cage dangling over a bottomless pit. Whatever the image, the feelings have similar characteristics. But this is not much comfort—to every depressed person the feelings of being cut off from every other human being are stark and painful.

Why didn't anyone tell me that life could be like this?

You do not have to be very depressed to realize that there are only a perceptive few who see your pain, but they may well not know what to do or say. The others, sadly often your closest relatives, friends, sometimes even your doctor, will insist that you get a grip on yourself, 'snap out of it' and get on with living.

It is then that your world takes on the ghastly reality of the isolation of the depressed. You know that no other human being can have felt like this because someone would have told you—warned you that it could be this bad. But the experience cannot be put into words or communicated. You are right that no one else ever felt like this because each depression is its own unique self. It takes on a life of its own. It has its own root causes peculiar to you.

19

**And nothing to look backward to with pride
And nothing to look forward to with hope.**

Robert Frost

You ask for help and they stuff you with pills. They won't listen because you need a million hours. You need a million hugs. You need a million words of reassurance.

These you cannot have, for the world is busy with its own life and importance. The reality is that you are what the world might call 'mentally ill'. And that reality hurts. It hurts like hell.

People who make out there are simple answers are wrong, and their cliché-ridden talk drives you further into depression.

Now I am setting out into the unknown. It will take me a long while to work through the grief. There are no shortcuts; it has to be gone through.

Madeleine L'Engle

4

Finding the cave: ideas for the very bad days
We only think when we are confronted with a problem.

John Dewey

From where you are there may seem to be no footholds, no roots to hold on to. No one is around with a rope. It's pitch dark. The rock is jagged. It is slippery with seaweed. Every time you make a move you get wet feet.

You are tired. Hungry. Cold. Utterly miserable and incapable of even looking at the cliff, never mind attempting to climb it.

One bit of you doesn't care a jot about the fact that any moment now the tide will wash you away, but some little spark in there prompts you to remember that before the sun set, you saw a cave. Just over to the left. If you went now, maybe you would make it. It isn't far. At least it would be warmer.

I have called the first step out of depression 'finding the cave'. It's not the top of the hill; it's a long way from where we want to end up. But it keeps us from being washed away by the tide. This is what I mean:

1 Do something!

You're reading this book, so that will do for a start. Don't aim too high. Make a cup of tea, or switch on the radio.

On better days it may be appropriate to ask yourself why you feel this bad today. What are you actually feeling? But I don't do that on the worst days. I just try to exist for the next ten minutes, then the next . . .

2 Find your 'cave'—at least it will be warm and dry

My 'cave' is my bed. I get under the quilt with my cuddly toy and refuse to come out for hours (it used to be days) on end. For some people the 'cave' is watching the television, reading, cooking, or walking. It doesn't matter where we escape to. It is important that we escape from the pressures of our world and do something that pleases us enough to stop the crying and the spiralling down into total oblivion.

For me, part of the 'escape' is absorbing myself in stories— either my own or those of others. I get into the world of the story and leave the other world behind for a bit. I feel safe in my own world. Once I feel safe I can think of coming out of my 'cave'.

It is vital to recognize at this stage that if crawling under the quilt is all you can manage to do, *don't feel guilty about it! That will only make you feel worse*.

Anyone near you, your family for example, may well need training in recognizing that retreating to your cave is all you are capable of. They won't necessarily understand. They will almost certainly be irritated at your apparent self-centredness.

Yes, everything they say just makes it worse. That's how it is with depression. It is such a shock to every human being who experiences it exactly because it is almost impossible to communicate the paralyzingly dreadful feeling to anyone else. Each depressed person wonders why they are going through something that is so devastatingly painful that the thought of death is almost a comfort.

So find your 'cave'. Get into it, and stay there. Your family will *not* starve without you there for a while. The company will *not* grind to a halt. The world will *not* come to an end because you retreat to your bed. You are *not* actually indispensable, and at the moment you maybe have to allow yourself to be a little bit self-protective. A basic rule for a depressed person is 'be kind to yourself'.

3 Realize that these very worst moments do actually pass

If you can recognize at all that now is a little better than, say, four o'clock this morning, a crucial skill in surviving human existence is within your grasp. *Everything in the world as we know it comes to an end*. Good things. Bad things. They all end. These feelings will, one day, not be there. But today they are there and they hurt.

If we are going to think positively about climbing the cliff, it helps to know what's going on in our minds and emotions when we are at the bottom. Somehow we need to understand what our pain is trying to tell us. What is it that is underneath our depression?

◆ It is a surprisingly common human experience to be at the bottom of the cliff in utter depression.

◆ It is not your 'fault' or anything to feel guilty about.

◆ It is not something you can just 'snap out of'—despite what people say!

> **My life as an actor has been a form of therapy ... [It has allowed me] to free myself of some unutterable burden.**
> **Anthony Hopkins**

In the next chapters we will look at **what depression is** and **some of the possible causes** of depression.

5

What is depression?
Depression is the worst non-physical pain known to humans.

A doctor

One of the most striking things about depression is its horrifying inevitability. Quite frankly I just don't believe those who say they have never had a day of depression in their lives! I think it more likely either that they deny the strength of their feelings—perhaps because they cannot cope with them—or that they are just not able to recognize the symptoms!

There are different levels of depression. Many people who are depressed get better on their own, but feeling low can escalate and some of us are all too familiar with the confusion and hopelessness that can characterize a deeper depression. Doctors regard this as an illness and sometimes may treat it with drugs, electro-convulsive therapy (ECT), or with a talking treatment—therapy or counselling.

Some of us experience depression so severely that our lives are changed significantly as we struggle to find some meaning and purpose. When the depression lifts we know that we will never be the same person again. It will always leave a scar. Paradoxically though, it may be that we will be left more 'whole' than we were before—more of a 'full' human being.

Severe depression is being recognized as one of the major health concerns of this century.

Dr Richard Winter

I'm told that depression affects almost every culture throughout the world. Some people think that there is more of it sophisticated cultures, and that seems to make a lot of sense. We know, though, that it is not just modern life that provokes depression. The Greek physician Hippocrates described it four hundred years before Jesus lived.

The list of famous depressives is very reassuring! It includes

Beethoven, Schumann, William Cowper, Isaac Newton, Franz Kafka, Darwin, Tolstoy, Winston Churchill (he called it his 'black dog'), and two of my favourite twentieth-century comedians, Tony Hancock and Spike Milligan.

For some, one particular form of depressive illness can have some advantages. It is what doctors call manic depression, characterized by extreme mood swings. As well as times of deepest melancholy there are also times of elation. On a 'high' the person can be so creative and engage in such intense activity that their level of achievement is very great. I'm told that many inventors did their best work in these manic phases. It is not surprising, therefore, that it is sometimes said that genius is close to 'mental illness'.

The other side of the story, though, is that often during a 'high' a project which is totally unrealistic, and cannot be completed, is started. There isn't the cash to pay for it. There isn't the expertise to carry the plans out. This results in further depression.

Many writers, artists and particularly poets are likely to experience depression. I find this very comforting, and it certainly rings true to my experience—many of the depressed people I meet tend to be very sensitive and creative.

Different kinds of depression

There is a set of labels for depressed people who go to the doctor's surgery. For example, a person who has symptoms of depression, such as sleeplessness and a loss of interest in anything, but who otherwise seems to have no problems might be given the label 'endogenous depression'. A person whose depression is mostly a response to very difficult circumstances, such as bereavement, might be said to have 'reactive depression'.

Some doctors seem to love labels! One problem I have noticed, though, is that if the same person goes to a different doctor, they might get a different label! If they went to someone not trained in medicine but in psychology, or in therapy, they might not get a label at all (or any medication).

We need to be a little bit cautious about labels. There are quite a lot of them. Here are some:

endogenous depression

reactive depression

manic depression

cyclic depression

post-natal depression

anxiety state.

There are many more. They are probably Deeply Meaningful, but they may well not tell the whole truth. The first two labels are quite common.

Endogenous depression

This means that the depression is thought of as coming from within the person, and for many doctors it indicates some kind of imbalance in the body chemistry. For others, such as psychotherapists, however, if there is no obvious reason for depression it might signal that there are causes which are still covered up. These may be from childhood, from bereavement or from some other unresolved trauma.

Some therapists use a 'talking therapy' to approach this kind of depression. Some doctors might correct the imbalance in the body with some kind of medication. Some of us benefit from both therapy and medication.

My personal belief is that those who think that 'endogenous depression' has no cause other than body chemistry are not usually seeing the whole story. It may be a depression where the story has yet to be told. I lived with the label for years. It made me feel so helpless, yet it made me passive. 'There is nothing I can do about this. I'm ill.' Then I had some help from a psychologist who said, 'Tell me your story'. That was the beginning of my climb up out of depression.

Reactive depression

Depression is very often a reaction to events or circumstances. If important things happen to us, we react. The death of someone we love, or the thought of leaving our home, or the news that we, or a friend, have got cancer can cause us to plummet down into despair.

Some of that despair can be about trying to contain our unrecognized rage. How could that so-called 'God of love' let such a lovely person get cancer? The despair can also be about fear:

People the same age as me are dying.

I won't know anyone in the new town.

When my children leave home I will feel all alone.

All these things are the stuff of potential depression. We can't cope with them so we retreat into 'reactive' depression instead.

Children who have suffered sustained periods of pain repress trauma in order to survive. This repressed emotion sows the seed from which later depression will come.

Anti-depressant medication

Whatever kind your depression is, it is important to see your doctor. He may well offer some medication; I have found it a life-saver.

There are several different types of anti-depressant drugs and it is often a case of finding the one that will suit you the best. They take several days to take effect, so swapping from one to another may mean an agonizingly long time before the tablets can work. But it may be worth persevering. Although I don't think drugs are the answer, they can lift the mood so that life can be coped with, and the real causes worked at.

A 'person' not a 'case'

What gave me my first insight into the idea that doctors and psychiatrists might not always be right with their labels was that each one I saw gave me a different one. I've had most of those listed above! Not only was that really mind-blowingly funny, it was utterly disconcerting. I didn't see myself as a 'cyclic depressive with paranoid tendencies' (eh?).

I was a hurting person and I wanted to know why. I thought if I understood my hurt I could get better and go back home and look after my babies.

Being given a label and being treated with pills, injections and electrodes seemed not to address me as a human being. I never found pills or electrodes particularly therapeutic. They controlled me. They made me passive. They stopped me expressing my stress. Gradually, with medication and ECT, I would feel better (which was wonderful) and then I would be allowed home. Then if things got bad again, it would start all over again.

I don't mean at all that psychiatrists, or doctors, or drugs, are no help to anyone. On the contrary, it is very important to be in touch with your doctor if your depression is serious. What I do mean is that for some depressed people the labels and the treatments that some doctors tend to give are not always relevant.

It was important for me to grow beyond the 'box' that some doctors wanted to put me in. (Woe betide me if I behaved in a way that my label didn't allow for!) My climb up out of depression has been a gradual process involving millions of words and a lot of hugs. In fact, the only label I needed was 'person'.

> Answer me, O Lord, out of the goodness of your love;
> in your great mercy turn to me.
> Do not hide your face from your servant;
> answer me quickly, for I am in trouble.
>
> **The psalmist**

6

What causes depression?
Most people get a fair amount of fun out of their lives, but on balance life is suffering, and only the very young or the very foolish imagine otherwise.

George Orwell

The first and most important thing to say about the causes of depression is that there is no one simple answer. The reasons for depression becoming a part of someone's life can be complex and extremely difficult to unravel. Some people can say exactly why they are depressed, but for others there is no obvious reason. Some reasons are a complex confusion of the past and present, and the twists and turns of the mind through a lifetime.

These complex factors are a series of things which make the feelings of mild depression escalate, unnervingly, rapidly downwards into a depression we may feel we never escape from. This section outlines some of these possible factors.

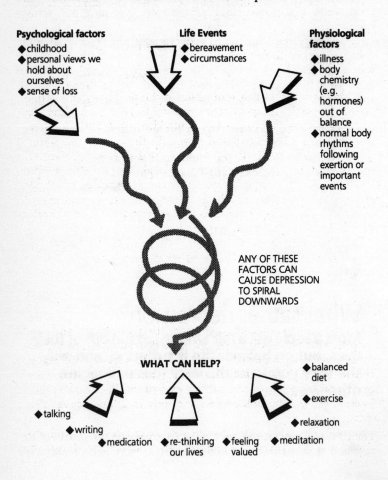

Psychological factors
- childhood
- personal views we hold about ourselves
- sense of loss

Life Events
- bereavement
- circumstances

Physiological factors
- illness
- body chemistry (e.g. hormones) out of balance
- normal body rhythms following exertion or important events

ANY OF THESE FACTORS CAN CAUSE DEPRESSION TO SPIRAL DOWNWARDS

WHAT CAN HELP?
- talking
- writing
- medication
- re-thinking our lives
- feeling valued
- balanced diet
- exercise
- relaxation
- meditation

Body chemistry out of balance?

There is a strong link between body chemistry and moods in both men and women. Many women recognize the raging tiger in themselves that emerges before their monthly period. Or, after childbirth, women clutch their newborn babies knowing that they are 'supposed' to be happy, but that all they really want to do is weep. Their hormones are all over the place. A flu or other virus can also leave us feeling miserable.

Other illnesses, especially long-term ones or those that took a lot out of us, can leave us depressed and unable to cope.

> **Depression, like the common cold, is no respecter of persons.**
>
> **Myra Chave-Jones**

Taking antibiotics can sometimes make us depressed. It may rob our bodies of things that are needed to keep us healthy (for example, we need microbes in our intestines to feel OK). There are chemicals in our food and drink, in the air, in the water, which can influence how our bodies are functioning. Farmers feel ill after putting their sheep through certain sheep dips. Hayfever sufferers can feel wretched when the pollen of oilseed rape is in the atmosphere. Alcohol—not necessarily a lot of it—is a depressant. Some people have unrecognized food allergies that can cause them to feel low.

These are the sorts of triggers that can lead to longer and intense depression, especially if other circumstances of life are not good.

Burnout

When my children became teenagers, they became moody and low following any really big event. The crucial exams or the important concert seemed inevitably to lead to a feeling of flatness: 'Why ever did I put all that effort in? It wasn't that important and now I don't want to do anything except sit here and mope.' Maybe these are the times when our body is asking for rest after stress.

Burnout can happen to anyone who puts heart and soul into things. It is often seen as something that happens to those who work desperately hard over a long period of time, such as the young father who pushes himself at work and then goes home to the stresses of a family. The depression that often comes with that is perhaps a very 'healthy' reaction for the body to make.

Childhood

Reactive depression often comes from responses made in childhood. As little children we were unable to understand the world, and we inevitably got our climbing ropes all confused.

Childhood doesn't have to have been particularly traumatic for someone to carry scars into adult life. Often, quite unintentionally, a parent can give a child the message that she is not valued just for who she is. Love becomes conditional: 'If you are a good boy like Tom next door . . .'; 'We love you when . . .'; 'You have to get straight 'A's for us to really love you and approve of you.'

It is not necessarily the apparently important things which affect a child—he may misinterpret the seemingly insignificant: 'Daddy doesn't love me because he said he would read me a story, but then the phone rang and he went downstairs.' If he feels of less value than a phone call, he will easily come to believe that he is of little value.

It's always winter and never Christmas.
Mr Tumnus in The Lion, the Witch and the Wardrobe, **C.S. Lewis**

Depression and lifestyle

Some people's circumstances are problematic and depressing. Sometimes, in some extraordinary way, we can repeat difficult experiences from our childhood in adult life. It is said, for example, that we tend to parent our children in the way that we were parented. (Of course, that is not always true.)

Sometimes it seems that we *need* to keep hold of childhood problems. For example, the daughter of an abusive alcoholic may marry a similar man herself, and so repeat the problem. People can get trapped in ongoing patterns of behaviour.

Depression and personality

There may be things in an individual's life that are difficult or impossible to change, and this affects them severely. I think if I lived in a famine-stricken country I would be pretty depressed! It can also be that someone's personality tends towards the gloomy. Take Puddleglum, for example, in *The Silver Chair* by C.S. Lewis, or Eeyore—quite the most gloomy character in children's fiction—who lived in the Hundred Acre Wood with Christopher Robin. There would be absolutely no point in telling either of them to cheer up. It just isn't in their nature to be like that!

Some people are like that too. It doesn't mean, though, that we need to spend our whole lives in total misery. It just might be that for some of us, life will always seem problematic and gloomy.

Is depression hereditary—can I pass it on to my child? It would seem that any child who grows up with at least one parent depressed might well develop a depressing view of life. But it can develop in many ways—being bullied at school year after year, feeling unloved and rejected by a parent—many things are able to make a child become depressed. It is hard to know if it is 'nature' (they are born that way) or 'nurture' (they become that way through circumstances).

Depression and loss

To lose an object of significance is a depressing event. If our house is repossessed because we can't keep up the payments, or if we lose a precious possession, we are naturally upset. To lose a person through death, or desertion, or some kind of separation, is often very much harder to deal with than the loss of a material object.

There are other kinds of loss though, and they are much more difficult to get a grip on. Much of my own depression was a loss of self-esteem. I thought I was of no value. If I feel I have no value then I have no place in the world. If I don't think I belong I will feel insecure. It is impossible to function successfully in the world with these kinds of losses dominating our thoughts.

31

Depression and guilt

For me, guilt is one of the hardest things to face in depression. When I talk to others who are depressed, guilt invariably comes onto the agenda. I can see that much of others' guilt is unnecessary. They are just being over-sensitive. When it comes to my own guilt, I 'know' that it is real!

Guilt is very complex. It's not at all easy to see where it comes from. Of course, some guilt is real, and necessary. If we really have hurt someone, for example, we may still feel guilty even after we've said sorry. If we deal with it by pushing it deep down inside ourselves, danger lies ahead.

There is something about perfectionism that induces guilt. I know women who feel guilty if they don't do the washing up straight after a meal, or if there is a speck of dust in the house, or if the meal is not ready when the family want it. People who come to my house can see that I am far from a perfectionist in that sense. But it is important to recognize that there is a kind of perfectionism that can really get to us and go unrecognized for what it is. We sometimes—maybe even unknowingly—set ourselves impossible standards. Sometimes we feel guilty when we are not really guilty.

Depression and anger

Depression can be seen as a reverse side of anger. Myra Chave-Jones describes it as 'frozen rage' in her book *Coping with Depression*. That makes a lot of sense to me and every single depressed person I have talked to in any depth. We do not feel safe enough to express our anger so we suppress it. Our bodies try to contain that internalized anger but they fail and depression (or an ulcer or a heart attack) is the result.

Depression and the stresses of life

Going through a divorce, moving house, having problems at work or with kids is enough to make anyone feel that life is too much. The key to recovering from depression which is related to stress is to recognize our stress level and then plan a phase of recovery. (We will work at planning for recovery later on—in part 4.)

32

However, the laws of the universe being as they are, this will be the year gran dies, our neighbour gets cancer and a new five-lane motorway is built at the end of our garden.

Depression and women

More women than men get depressed. There could be many reasons for this, such as hormone imbalances with periods, pregnancy and so on.

But a woman gets it wrong whatever she does. If she stays at home to look after her baby she is boring. If she goes to work and parks the children out at the local day nursery, she is a terrible mother. Even if no one actually says that, that's what we tell ourselves! Guilt that we didn't do it right as a mother, lover, friend, colleague and person comes to the surface easily.

If we try to break out of the mould that society makes for women then our troubles really start! I don't have any answers to this. But it is interesting that women sometimes seem to be the dumping ground for so many of the ills of society. Those problems not caused by mothers are caused by teachers, so as a teacher and mother I get it both ways!

I read in a newspaper about some research where it was found that if women go to a doctor with a symptom such as a pounding heart, it is likely they will be given tranquillisers and anti-depressants. However, if men complain of identical symptoms, they will be more likely to be referred for a heart complaint. I suppose men are meant to be tough and macho and not get depressed or anxious. I think that must be incredibly hard to deal with for a man who is depressed.

Depression is complicated

Depression leaves precious little in reserve to face the daily knocks of life. It is the anniversary of a death, it's raining, you still feel a bit wobbly from a tummy bug. Burning the toast is then a major disaster and you spiral downwards.

Things which previously did not bother us come to the surface and hurt. The depression following redundancy is not necessarily just about that rejection. Similar pain in childhood may surface and need to be worked through.

33

Maybe the only thing that we can say with certainty about depression is that it is mindbogglingly complicated!

The causes of depression are complex, and an important part of our climb up is to try to understand the reasons why we are sitting at the foot of the cliff. We need to 'hear' what our body is trying to tell us and uncover buried memories. Sorting out those reasons is not easy. It's not comfortable, and it can't be done overnight. But this book is about having a go.

▓ Activity

Here are some first steps:

⤳ Draw a diagram like the one in chapter 6 . Try to put on some of the things that have caused you to lose your grip on life.

⤳ Start to tell your own story. You could do this by making an overall sketch of critical events. What were the really important moments for you?

A journey of a thousand miles begins with a single step.

For more on **negative thinking** see chapter 18; **losses**, chapter 26; **anger**, chapter 22; **guilt**, chapter 23; **stress**, chapter 27; the **'goodenough' principle**, chapter 9.

7

Being kind to ourselves
It may be that those who do most, dream most.
Stephen Leacock

When you are depressed it is hard to be kind to yourself. You tend to run yourself down, to focus on negative characteristics

('I'm no good at . . .') and to feel in some spectacularly odd way that this depression is deserved.

We need to learn to be kind to ourselves both at the bottom of the cliff and as we undertake the climb up. How do we learn to be kind to ourselves?

◆ With difficulty! Especially if we believe that somehow we deserve this 'punishment'. That is just part of the evidence that God is fed up with us and has chosen to throw a thunderbolt of depression our way.

◆ Be realistic. No one gets better from depression in a day, by pushing themselves beyond what they are able to do, or by sitting around moaning or telling themselves that things must be perfect. These things tend to cause us to slither down the cliff even further.

◆ Accept what is happening. Persistently refusing to believe we are actually depressed, or feeling guilty that it is happening, or not acknowledging how much it hurts will only delay the climb up the cliff face.

◆ Be patient. We don't usually get to the top of the climb just by wanting to be there. That 'wanting' is a great start, but the actual climb takes time and effort. It is like dieting. Patience is a key word. Lose weight fast and it will go back on the minute you dive for the chocolate. In the same way the best plan for dealing with depression is the long-term plan.

◆ Get plenty of rest. Many of us experience overwhelming tiredness when we are depressed. This gets very mixed up with feelings that it isn't worth doing anything anyway. So we may not always appreciate that this tiredness may well be a complex mixture of despair, exhausting anxiety and stress. We need plenty of sleep, but sleep is sometimes difficult in depression. Taking tablets to help sleep is OK for the really bad times.

◆ Get plenty of exercise. Surprisingly, although we often feel exhausted by being awake for ten minutes, getting some exercise can make us feel less tired. It relieves stress too. But go gently.

◆ Do things you enjoy. It isn't selfish to take ourselves out for the day to go bird-watching, or to the cinema. It is all part of our survival strategy, and everyone needs one.

◆ Take a break from caring for the baby if you have post-natal depression. Teaming up with another mum may help. You can take it in turns to be child-free. The baby will be fine. We are better mothers if we take a break!

Blessed are you who weep now, for you will laugh.
Jesus, from the Gospel of Matthew

▨ Activity

What can I do to be kind to myself today?

⤳ List the things you like doing. Put the list up where you will see it. Add to it when you think of other good things.

⤳ Make time to do some of the things!

This section was all about the reasons why we might be sitting at the foot of the cliff in depression. The next section looks at the issues involved if we are going to think about **climbing up** out of depression.

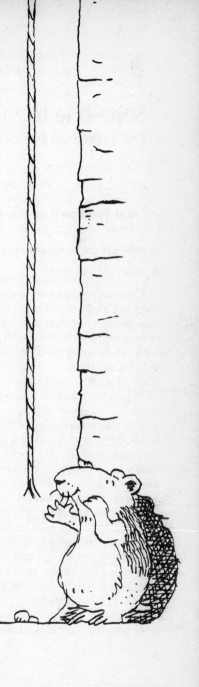

PART 3

IS CLIMBING
FOR ME?

8

Someone to talk to
I'm a spiritual person and prayer is useful.

Madonna

If we are going to think about climbing up out of depression, there will be many questions that need answering. Climbing out of depression is as difficult and demanding as climbing up a cliff face.

◆ Am I sure that it will be worth the effort?

◆ What will it be like?

If we decide to climb up, there are several things that we need. First we're going to need someone to talk to. Actually finding this person, someone who really understands, is incredibly reassuring. Maybe that is why 'talking therapies' seem to work so well in helping people out of depression. Making a deep relationship with someone is a healing thing—there is someone there. I'm not totally alone. Someone values me.

When we speak out our confused muddle of hopelessness and despair, the greatest gift we can be given is to have it handled gently and sensitively. When someone takes our ramblings and holds them with great tenderness, like an injured butterfly, we feel understood. The world seems a less frightening place. They don't have to speak because we do not always need words to comfort us. It is more the look in their eyes, that acceptance of us as a person, where we are. It makes the dreadful searing pain that we try so desperately, and always inadequately, to express, seem shared and therefore a little more bearable.

For a few moments the pain and the dreadful loneliness recede. We feel a tug on the lifeline. It makes a silent impact on our body. We have connected with a human being. Something in our inner world feels strengthened. A basic human need is satisfied, albeit briefly.

Although we can do some bits of the climb on our own, it is very much better if we have someone to talk to.

Too many cooks...?

But this sharing can also lead us into places of the greatest danger. Knowing that we need this human compassion and sharing, we can open ourselves up unwisely. Sometimes we talk to too many people. Maybe it is the belief that if we share something of it all with enough people, one of them will understand.

Trying to talk to and rely on lots of people is dangerous. A case of 'too many lifeline holders spoil the climb'. Our indecision as to who will hold the lifeline could leave people unsure whether they should be bracing themselves for a fall.

If we talk to too many people it can also make us rather superficial. Trying to express our fears and loneliness to just one trusted friend will help up to go deeper into the problem. Expressing it to six means we stay superficial. That's probably why we do it.

Trusting

To find a special friend is a gift. But it is not a gift that is easy to receive. It is very difficult to accept it, and it involves great trust. However, if we are going to climb successfully we do need to find someone we can trust.

If we attempt the climb relying on one person's grip on the lifeline, they may well let us down. We know that. If we slip and put all our weight on it we are totally dependent on them bracing themselves. We rely on their ability to grip the rope as it runs through their fingers.

As we sit at the bottom of the cliff contemplating the climb we may not be able to take that risk. There may be no one, no human being that at the moment we feel we could trust with the lifeline.

There are lots of bits of the climb that come down to trusting. The leader's voice from below yells out that there is a handhold out of sight up to the left. When we try a tricky move we are trusting in the lifeline and the strength of the person below holding onto the other end if we fall. We often follow instructions blindly, believing and trusting that the advice of our leader will be right.

If we are going to climb, we need to think about who we are going to trust.

⤳ Who do I trust?

⤳ Who could I learn to trust?

To reveal myself openly and honestly takes the rawest kind of courage.

John Powell

Information about **choosing a therapist** in chapter 11.

9

The 'goodenough' principle
Depression is without doubt the most unpleasant experience known to man.

A doctor

Another thing that we will have to learn if we are going to climb is the 'goodenough' principle. (The phrase comes from the psychologist D.W. Winnicott.)

The idea of being 'goodenough' has helped me enormously over the years of depression, through motherhood, throughout my professional life and into mid-life. This 'goodenough' principle is that what we have done—at work, home, in the garden or wherever, may not be fantastically wonderful, it may not be perfect, it may not even be the best that we could do, but is it good enough?

Will it do? That is the real question.

Those of us who have a perfectionist streak, or who do not believe in ourselves very much, or who have so much to do that we just can't do things as well as we would like, can revolutionize our lives if we can grasp the 'goodenough' principle. If you:

◆ constantly look at the dust and tell yourself how bad you are at housework

◆ look at the kids and think you should be taking them to the park and doing something Deeply Meaningful with them

◆ get a pie out of the oven and think how badly you have made it

◆ go into work on your day off

◆ always measure yourself by some external benchmark, such as trying to be as good a cook as your mother-in-law, or as good at your job as the guy in the next office . . .

. . . you need to rethink things.

Is it goodenough?

The idea 'is it goodenough?' is a great rescuer.

◆ I may not be a perfect parent, but the kids are happy, so maybe I'm goodenough.

◆ I may not be doing this job as well as I could be if things were different, but it's goodenough.

◆ I may not be the best cook in the world, but it's OK enough to eat.

◆ I may not be putting up these shelves particularly well, but they will be straight enough.

◆ I may not be as good at this as Charlie, but I'm goodenough.

Changing our standards

Trying to do things perfectly can sometimes mean that we do them less well. Can I learn to accept that doing it well enough is OK? Sometimes my standards (or other people's) are not realistic.

Why does it matter to me to be a fantastic mother/worker/boss/Christian/patient/partner/daughter/son?

> I was trundling around with all my inadequacies and inner pain and loneliness and I yearned, desperately, to be something. I yearned to get out from where I was... some deep discontent within myself, actually some deep dislike of myself.
>
> **Anthony Hopkins**

 Activity

↝ Identify what seems not to be 'goodenough'.

↝ Work on the idea of being 'goodenough'.

More about: **being 'goodenough'** in chapter 9 .

10

Strategies for living
Pain is a teacher from whom we can learn much.
John Powell

We need to learn some strategies for living. It's not just the bad days that need some kind of plan of action. We will climb better if we have some general strategies for every day.

I had no strategies for living before I was depressed. It was all a very hit-or-miss affair. As the bad times and crises came I was pushed around and tossed from one thing to the next. I never felt I had any control over my life. Whatever came at me hit me full in the face and it seemed as if I could do nothing about it.

Now, I steer myself through the bad times much more. Instead of falling at the first sign of trouble, I find a place of refuge. As the debris falls off the cliff face, I seem to be able to duck.

Each crisis and down time (and there are plenty of them!) is now something of a challenge. With this sense of being in more overall control, I almost watch myself handle it. That's a bit odd, but it gives me an enormous sense of achievement, even if my stomach does continue to lurch and my body cries out for valium.

As disaster strikes now and I feel the panic rising, I know . . .

◆ I have been here so often before that I will get through it just like last time

◆ My clinging-on skills get better every time

◆ I now have a plan for the difficult times.

As I write this I know that my foothold feels extraordinarily insecure and crumbly, and I sense that any moment I may fall off. I look at all this positive stuff I'm writing and it is very far from the way it actually feels at the moment. But somehow I have survived enough to help me believe that I may just be given the strength to hold on. Each time I survive it seems to strengthen my ability to grip onto the cliff face.

Suffering can be used creatively.

Susan Howatch

The trouble is that we cannot control some things. They hit us just because they are there. Today I learned of the death of a friend's son, at twenty-five. As I watch the news on the television, families weep for their loved ones.

When we hear these things we are certain that we would never cope if it happened to us. We hardly dare face our real emotions. If it were my my child who had died, I feel that I would simply curl up and die myself.

Yet one of the strategies for living is not to live in the world of 'what would happen if . . .' because gradually we learn that we somehow find the strength to face things. As a friend said to me about the death of her baby son, 'You are given the strength when it happens, and then just enough for each day at a time.'

'What if' and 'if only'

'What if' and 'if only' are phrases in the 'self-talk' in our heads that we constantly need to watch out for. They are almost always negative ways of thinking. (More about **negative thinking** in chapter 18.)

We'll need a mask for survival

Every man has three characters—that which he exhibits, that which he has, and that which he thinks he has.
Alphouse Karr (1808–90)

There is an image of a depressed person as someone who never smiles, or mopes about unable to do anything. For some that is how it is some of the time, but for others it is easy to laugh and to seem cheerful—and actually to be cheerful. Depressed people still have their sense of humour, and laughter is a good way of escaping. And it can be an important part of our mask that we present to the world.

Developing a mask is not always a bad thing. It can be an important survival strategy. A mask has a good side and a bad side.

The good side of the mask
We learn that if we behave in a cheerful way we somehow begin to feel our spirits lift. If we make the effort and actually manage to get ourselves out of the house in the morning and get on with our lives, we find to our astonishment that we can do it. It really isn't as bad as we thought it would be. (Usually!) The day as we imagine it at four in the morning does not seem as bad at four in the afternoon when we have done most of it. (Of course, there are some days which are so terrifyingly dreadful that we wish we had not made the effort.)

Someone once told me that you can become how you behave—'happiness is a choice' and all that. I thought that unbelievably stupid at the time. It would seem though that there is some truth in it.

The bad side of the mask
We can hide behind it and never face the truth of what we are really feeling. Many of us spend most of our lives doing that. We pretend that we are not frightened. We pretend that we are confident. We put on a brave face. We bury our emotions.

44

Buried emotions

We need to unearth our buried emotions. We have buried them alive, and they eventually struggle free. As these emotions emerge, we cannot recognize them for what they are. We have buried them for so long we have forgotten where they fit in. So the childhood emotion of the fear of being left alone breaks free at a time of crisis. But we don't express it as fear. Instead we become confused by our emotional state and perhaps hit out at someone we love. The fear has turned to aggression.

'Men don't cry,' I hear a mother at school say to her five year old—and he hides his real feelings. The hurt little boy retreats. It is never a surprise to me that the dear child that first comes to school is quite a thug by the time he is nine. Those hurt and angry feelings are still inside him somewhere. Someone could have hugged them away when he was five, but they didn't. Letting him scream and cry may have been a good thing because at least he would be expressing what he was really feeling *at the time he was feeling it*.

Now the feelings are all mixed up. Aggression seems to come from nowhere. It seems unrelated to the thing that caused it.

A man cannot possibly be at peace with others until he has learned to be at peace with himself.
Bertrand Russell

Most of us are aware of burying emotions. The 'difficult' teenager may well be rebelling against something that happened when she was seven. An outburst of temper in the family today could be the result of something yesterday, or last year, that wasn't recognized as stressful at the time, and so wasn't expressed.

Our depression is often about these buried feelings struggling to be recognized. If we are going to decide that 'climbing is for me', we are going to have to work at coming to terms with them.

There are two kinds of pain that we forget. We forget hurts too trivial to bother about. We forget pains too horrible for our memory to manage.
Lewis Smedes

Think

When we catch ourselves behaving unexpectedly we can get clues to our buried emotions.

Why do I feel so tense at the thought of that particular person coming to visit?

Why did I get so angry at such a trivial thing?

Why did I get that panic attack just then?

Activity

There all sorts of relaxation techniques on the market. It is a case of finding out what is best for you. I find the following sequence works well for me:

~→ 1 Doing some gentle exercise, if I feel up to it.

~→ 2 Listening to soothing music.

~→ 3 Taking a few slow deep breaths.

~→ 4 Lying on the floor or the bed and tensing up every part of the body in turn. Start by tensing the feet and legs, hold for a few seconds, then let go. Then tense the muscles around the hips, hold and let go. Gradually work at each area of the body, not forgetting to include the neck and the face.

~→ On days when I have more time, I break the tensing down into smaller units—feet, calf muscles, knees and so on, all separately.

~→ 5 End by tensing up every muscle you possibly can, hold, then let go.

~→ 6 Repeat sequence from 3 if you are still finding it hard to relax.

~→ 7 When the muscles are relaxed, just lie quietly. Listen to the music and thinking of good things, for example watching the sun set over the sea.

~→ If you find worries start creeping into your mind, try focusing on something positive and good—pictures, the

46

music, or some progress you've made. Even on days when the worries don't go away, just a few minutes of 'goodenough' relaxation is helpful.

Doing this relaxation routine regularly makes you better at it and it is easier to recognize the early signs of tension as they creep in physically.

⤳ A long soothing bath is good on days when the worries crowd in thick and fast. I've tried some of the aromatherapy relaxing oils available and they seem to help.

For relaxation during **panic attacks** see chapter 21.

11

What about professional therapy?
Every man passes his life in the search after friendship.

Emerson

Not all of us have a friend who will listen in the way that we need. Sometimes, even if we are deeply loved and befriended, we still need someone else to talk to—someone who is outside it all. Maybe this is the time to think about some professional counselling or therapy.

Choosing a therapist

I'm not qualified to talk about different kinds of therapy in any technical way. I can just describe how it has been for me and the people that I know. If you want to know more about specific types of therapy, for example what it means if someone is a 'cognitive' therapist, or if they follow Jung, I recommend Dorothy Rowe's book *Breaking the Bonds* (see resources list at the end of the book).

My own rules are:

◆ If it comes through the health service and does not cost a terrifying amount of money, it is at least worth a go.

◆ If the therapist is apparently kind (as opposed to sitting behind a desk in a white coat telling you how stupid you are) then it is also worth exploring further.

◆ If what is on offer is only medication, you may need something else as well.

◆ If they cost the earth, but seem helpful, don't get hooked on it. They may want you to stick around for a bit to pay their mortgage. Proceed with caution.

Surviving therapy

I have a few survival pointers for therapy. Going into it is not an easy option. Some think that it should be on the life events list for high stress (see chapter 27)—it would be pretty near the top!

It's tough, but if we can survive, it could be the most helpful thing that we could ever do to get out of depression. (No promises, of course.)

Here are my rules for survival.

◆ It takes enormous courage, so tell the therapist if you are terrified.

◆ Expect it to get very much worse before it gets better.

◆ Even if after ten agonizing sessions you still think that the therapist hates your guts, it may be worth going on—but tell them.

◆ If the therapist is clearly an insensitive idiot, get out, quickly.

◆ If the therapist tries to make connections between things that have been said—trying to get at what is underneath our talking—and these connections make absolutely no sense whatsoever to us, it's important to say so. If their reaction is then to search further, or to try another lead, that's a good sign.

48

If, on the other hand, the explanations sound like irrelevant garbage and we say so and we get put in our place and made to feel small, that may be a signal that the therapist needs therapy as much as we do! Rapid retreat could be called for if this persists. But it is crucial to explore it first with the therapist. It could well be a key issue.

◆ Don't just give up. Explore all problems widely.

◆ It might be that, if things go badly, we have unrealistic expectations. Explore this with the therapist.

◆ If most of what is said is jargon, it is a good idea to say so. If the response is a real attempt at communication, go on. But if it is that it is all our fault and 'shows clearly that blah blah blah gobbledegook gobbledegook, don't you think so, Sue?' I don't know what to suggest. I never really sussed that one out.

◆ All therapy is painful. It's not a good idea to give it up for that reason. However, it can be a good thing to stop if life gets so overwhelming that your survival is in doubt. There is a right time for things. We need to be ready to face things. There are also some approaches in therapy that may not be right for you at that time. It's OK to say you can't cope with it right now.

> There is a time for everything,
>   and a season for every activity under heaven:
>   a time to weep and a time to laugh,
>   a time to mourn and a time to dance,
>   a time to be silent and a time to speak.
>   **The writer of Ecclesiastes**

12

Preparing for the bad days
We thank thee that darkness reminds us of light.

T.S. Eliot

If we are at all realistic about life, we soon come to see that some days are much worse than others. If we prepare for the bad days, we can get through them much better and the whole journey seems a bit easier. Making the decision to try to climb up seems a more reasonable option.

I think of this as strategies for the overhang—the really difficult bits. My survival strategies won't be the same as yours, but the crucial thing is to make preparations on a good day for when it gets bad again.

My strategies for bad days include:

◆ having a list in my journal of things that I like doing

◆ making entries in my journal on good days—it's a help to read this on the bad days

◆ putting things by my bed that I enjoy and that lift my spirits, such as favourite books, poems and tapes, pictures and photos that remind me of the good times.

Being prepared for terrible thoughts

There are two particular things that really shook me when I was trying to decide whether to take the risk of climbing out of depression.

The first was what someone said to me once when I was very depressed: *Depression is not the worst thing in the world*. I thought that very silly. Of course depression is the worst thing in the world. Everyone knows that. (All sensible people anyway.)

But it isn't. It is the things that are behind the depression that are much worse. I call these things the Deeply Meaningful Something-or-others (DMSs). Finding out what our own DMSs are is one of the crucial things in our climb from depression.

Much of this book is about finding out what those things—the DMSs—behind depression are. Many people have particular ways of thinking or behaving that have developed from childhood, but which trap them in guilt, fear or anger. We have beliefs about ourselves and our circumstances that trap us in depression.

Many psychologists believe that the things that are behind depression are so difficult for us to face that we go into depression to escape from them.

I've had enough, Lord, take my life.

The prophet Elijah

It's a terrible thought that there is something worse than the living hell of depression. How can that possibly be? And if it is true, they—the Deeply Meaningful Something-or-others—must be horrendously terrible things if I escape from them into this!

The other really terrible thought is, as Dorothy Rowe puts it in her book *Depression, the Way out of your Prison*, that we hold the key to let ourselves out of our prison of depression. When I first read that book, I thought it was so ridiculous that I didn't read any further than the first page. I was irritated and extremely cross that anyone should suggest that all I have to do is to get up and let myself out of this hell-hole.

In my paranoid way I had turned it around and was saying, 'There you are—it's all your fault, all you have to do is get up and let yourself out—you are so pathetic.'

Dorothy Rowe isn't saying it's all our 'fault'. I had got it wrong. We do have the power (eventually) to get up (slowly and very painfully) from our depression. But it is not easy. It is not our 'fault'. We need courage and help to do it. We need comforters. We need a lot of time. We need to work hard at it.

Above all, we need to decide to set about changing our lives. An endless 'tomorrow will do' will get us nowhere.

Learning to be prepared to change

It is difficult to contemplate any kind of change in our lives. To contemplate it while we are experiencing the pain of depression is almost impossible. But if we are to get up the climb effectively then we do need to change. Otherwise life could go on being this terrible, with depression lurking ready to pounce on us at any moment.

> **The only sense that is common in the long run, is the sense of change—and we all instinctively avoid it.**
>
> **E.B. White**

Most change happens very slowly. Sometimes it takes years of patience for some very small thing to improve. It may not be our unwillingness to change, it may be not knowing how to change. I would gladly exchange the hell of depression for 'normal' life, but how?

How do we change?

The conditions that are right for change may well be different for every individual because depression is so very personal and varied. For me, much of the healing has come with time as I have grown to understand why I was depressed in the first place, and above all with having someone there beside me to help me.

When I became very depressed following the birth of my first longed-for baby, I was stuffed full of pills and talked at by psychiatrists and so on. Some of that may well have been of some help. I don't know. What really resolved it was realizing what lay behind the depression. The crunch was that I was only just able to cope with organizing my own rather fragile existence, trying as I was at that time to emerge from childhood and adolescent fears, fantasies and traumas.

Now though, I was responsible for this child I had willingly created. This caused childhood traumas to creep out from the graves in which I had buried them. So my life was even more fragile because I was trying to get up the climb still holding onto this infant who leaked at both ends at all times of the day and night.

I was exhausted. I would sit and ask myself questions that worried me deeply.

Will I be a terrible mother? How will I cope with the

52

responsibility of him as well as me? Will he suffer in the way I did? It's all too terrible to face. So I won't face it. I'll pretend it isn't there: Depression!

Facing the Deeply Meaningful Something-or-others

We would willingly exchange our depression for any other kind of pain. (Medieval instruments of torture seem insignificant beside depression. Give me tearing out of the fingernails any day.) But unfortunately we are not seeing the situation as it really is. Unless our depression is caused solely by some chemical imbalance in our bodies, the causes of it are buried deep in the tangle of our lives, our living circumstances, our loves and our hates, our dreams and our fantasies, our childhood horrors and the fears that lodge in the mind of any child, however well parented.

The right time

For some of us, it is simply not the right time to face up to what is behind it all. I'm sure, as I tried to free myself from depression, that I wanted to change. But I'm not sure that I understood why, or what to change to, and I certainly didn't understand how to change, even if I had the time to think about it, which I didn't. There were the nappies to wash (disposables in those days leaked and it got everywhere), the next feed to do, the baby clinic to go to and so on and so on.

My Deeply-Meaningful-Something-or-others that I know about now were not a part of my thinking in those days. How could I face them? You cannot free yourself from something if you don't know what it is. How can any of us possibly face up to recognizing our DMSs when life is so busy, and particularly when the depression is so bad that we question our basic wish to survive? If added to that we still do not really know who we are, we are unlikely to get a grip on our DMSs and get ourselves up out of the depression.

Men fear silence as they fear solitude, because both give them a glimpse of the terror of life's nothingness.
André Mauvois

I only faced my DMSs with someone who I trusted beside me, who loved me enough to listen. Someone who believed in me and also had the wisdom to help me to see what was underneath it all.

Those conditions for change are not always available. Most of us concentrate only on daily survival. It's like climbing. I go up a climb as well as I can. I don't have time to worry about style, or doing it by the book. I just do it. I trust the leader, and he holds the lifeline and shouts instructions. But I can't always follow them as he might expect. I just do *something*.

Change is possible

Dorothy Rowe makes the point that *we are not stuck with depression for ever*. We can do something about it. But we need to feel safe enough to face it all.

If we do decide we really must do something to change our situation, we also need to recognize that quite a big bit of us would prefer not to. Change is almost always rather frightening.

What helps us to change?

By getting the things in our mind out where we can recognize them, we can start to see what it is that makes us depressed. Tablets can never do that. However, taking some kind of medication can be a very good thing for some people.

Although I take anti-depressants, I don't leave it at that. I use them as a prop to make life tolerable while I try to unravel the chaos in my mind that made me depressed in the first place.

I want to know why it happened. I want to know what it is that I am really feeling. I want to stand there, poised on my toes trying to fathom out the next move. I'm less likely to fall back down the cliff if I get a firm grip, and if I don't rely on being dragged up.

If I can understand what made me depressed (again), then maybe I will be less likely to become depressed again in the future—or if I do get depressed again, maybe it will not be so bad.

My way to find out what my DMSs are is to write in my journal. This gives me time and space to find out what is worrying me. Your way might be to paint, or play loud music, or jog round the park.

Don't be put off by the thought that finding out what is behind the depression will be a very introspective process and that this is somehow a bad thing. I'm convinced that it is better to err on the side of too much introspection in order to find out what our DMSs are. Not to understand ourselves and to be depressed is infinitely worse than any risk of overdoing the thinking that a journal (or other creative activity) involves.

Finding time for quiet

Finding some time to ourselves in the day is a way of being quiet and listening to ourselves. We find it so hard to make the interminable racket in our minds shut down for long enough to latch on to the messages of love, of peace and of beauty that can come to us from our friends, or music or other things that we enjoy. To recover from depression we need to be quiet and to listen to ourselves. It is possible, even in this noisy world.

Much of the climb will be about discovering our inner selves—seeing our true value to our creator. There is growth towards learning to love ourselves. Not a narcissistic love—'Wow, I'm the greatest,' but a true love of our selves as valuable people in the world.

> **Most of my life I have needed more time to be on my own.**
> **P.D. James**

The journey towards this understanding of our inner selves, our 'heart and soul', takes many forms. I believe that relaxation and meditation can help us to get out of depression. It is not a case of meditating on 'nothing'—we have to choose what to meditate on.

My collection of pictures and poems that I keep by my bed helps me. I have a beautiful book of the psalms in a modern translation. The book has fantastic photos in it. They remind me of walking in the Yorkshire Dales with friends. That helps me to see beyond my feelings and into the beauty of the world. And when I look at my picture of a puffin, I think of the sea and the birds and freedom. That feels great.

My favourite picture is a little child protected by the hand of God. How I love that picture! I let myself feel like that little child, protected, loved and valued.

We need this type of thing in front of us to relax and meditate. By choosing these 'good' things, we are deciding that we want to be up at the top of the cliff.

55

What helps?

Looking back, the things that have helped me to get out of depressed phases have been

> **my friendship with someone who accepts me unconditionally, and is prepared to sit beside me and work with me in my struggle**

> **therapy**

> **praying with someone**

> **my own determination to do things to try to get better (talking, eating well, exercising and so on)**

> **finding time to be quiet and be on my own**

> **deciding that I want to be at the top of the cliff!**

Activity

↝ Take time to be quiet. Try the relaxation exercises in chapter 10, while listening to some beautiful music.

↝ If you are able to get out, go for a long walk in the country or park, or book an afternoon at a convent or monastery. It takes a bit of courage to ring up in the first place, but many of these places will welcome someone who just wants to sit and be quiet. You don't have to talk to anyone and you certainly don't have to be a churchgoer.

↝ Get ready a survival list for the bad days. Put pictures, tapes or whatever in a place where you can get to them easily (in a briefcase, pocket or bag, or on the mirror in the bathroom).

This section has been about some of the things that the climb up the cliff will involve. It's not easy. We are often tempted to give up. But the only way to make life any different is to decide to go for it. Ready?

> **Rock-bottom is not a nice place to live. But we have the consolation of knowing that there is only one way to go, and that is up.**
>
> **Ivy Rawkin Jeffers**

PART 4

FIRST STEPS

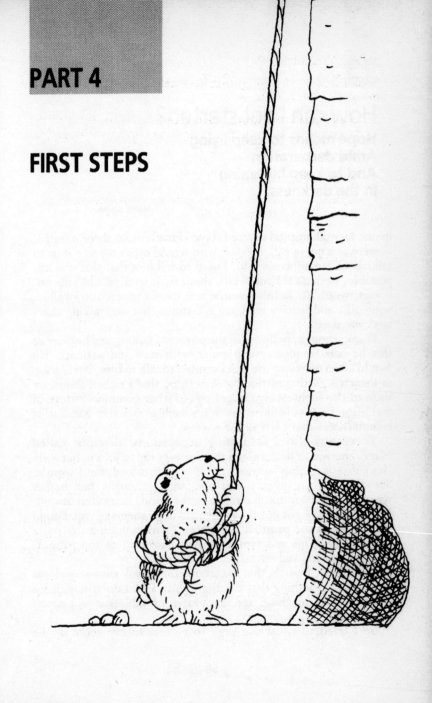

13

How can I get started?
Hope means to keep living
Amid desperation
And to keep humming
In the darkness.

Henri Nouwen

In one mental hospital where I stayed for a tedious three months, there was a nurse called Frank who would often try to get us to talk about our subconscious. I used to tell him that that was impossible, because if I could talk about it, it wouldn't be subconscious, would it? In this hospital you were expected to swallow your pills and behave well at ECT times, but no 'talking therapy' was used.

Frank, though, believed in the power of talking and because of this he was frequently unpopular with staff and patients. He would often convince me that I wanted to talk to him, but as soon as I started getting rattled by something that I talked about, or showed the slightest sign of crying (a rather common feature of my life), he would dose me with such a monster handful of tranquillisers that I felt ill for a week.

There was also a fascinating occupational therapist called Mary. She was as determined that I was going to join in her jolly 'let's do something' sessions as I was determined that I wasn't. She thought my poetry terrible, and I thought her basket weaving, and badminton outside in the wind, extremely stupid. But one day she got out the paints and huge sheets of paper and I wanted to sit and paint all afternoon. Frank wanted us to 'paint depression'. This was typical of him and most of the patients became puzzled and started to wander off.

I could see, though, that the talking that Frank encouraged was getting at something that the Big White Chief doctor with his electric buzz machine and his crates of tablets could never understand, or get near to.

So I tried to resist the urge to retreat to my room at the

thought of 'painting depression', and I sat for a while, trying to work out what Frank and Mary meant. Just three of us patients had remained at the painting table and we were nervously protesting that we didn't know what to do.

▓▓ Painting depression

Gradually we mixed our colours and tried things out, and threw first attempts away. We sank into silence. I can remember the feel of that silence, and being able to reach down into some part of me that I was not aware of. I remember asking myself what I *wanted* to paint. Having had a quite wonderful art teacher at school, I knew it was important that I painted something that mattered to me at that moment.

Elsie was painting flowers because they made her feel happy and reminded her of life as a child in Dorset. Mark was painting his house because he wanted to go home.

I couldn't settle to anything. I shut out Frank's questions and proddings and tried to think what it was that was inside me that I could express in painting. It felt as if everything was shrouded in darkness, so I began to paint darkness. I realized that I just wanted to paint in black. I was embarrassed by this. Somehow I wanted to paint a black hole. I wanted to paint nothingness. I wanted to try to get this devastating isolation out onto paper.

It felt as if the end of the world had come. I remember sitting weeping helplessly on the end of the bed, feeling more ill than I had ever felt in my life, and quite unable to face the thought of anything, or to cope with my father's death and possibly another miscarriage. I just wanted to be dead myself.

Susan Hill, Family

So I covered the whole paper in black. Then I tried again and painted huge black swirls covering most of the paper except a tiny hole in the middle. Annette, my best friend on the ward, had come back to the painting to join us by then and she was sharing my pot of black and painting huge figures on her paper. Frank was trying to talk to us, but neither of us would come out of our black holes. We just painted silently.

I sat for ages trying to work out if I wanted to put anything in my tiny little hole in the middle. I liked it empty because that was how it felt. A huge black hole with just a tiny speck of light—but that wasn't exactly right. I tried some other pictures. I did a deep dark pit with me sitting at the bottom unable to get out (all in black) and then another page that was meant to be my children but ended up as a page of outer space. I knew all the time that I had to go back to my tiny hole in the earlier painting.

It took a long time to work out what was needed in that hole. In the end I put a very simple Christian symbol, a cross. That felt right. It was a horrible dark isolated hole, in which there seemed no way out. But I had some vague hope in a God somewhere up there. If all that stuff I learned about at school meant anything, that was God's big moment to do something. I didn't know what I expected to happen, but that painting meant so much to me.

Still some hope?

It clarified for me that at least I still had hope. It wasn't a hope in myself. It certainly wasn't a hope in the hospital, or in Frank and his little chats about the subconscious. It was vague and intangible. I still felt utterly isolated. But there was the cross.

As I sat in silence beside my painting, I could see that I had made some kind of progress that afternoon. I understood myself and the depression a bit better. It felt an enormous relief.

Frank then decided it was the moment to interpret our paintings. He said that my black hole showed that I had 'religious overtones' to my life and because I had left that little hole in the middle, it showed that I wasn't really all that depressed! Annette's paintings were similarly subjected to this artistic critisism.

We both started to laugh, which just made Frank more bossy and (we thought) even more 'Freudian'. Mary told us to clear up and Frank was still discussing my painting with her. I didn't want them to do that. I had painted a bit of me onto that paper. I had tried to communicate. I now felt exposed and vulnerable.

I started to sob as I washed up the brushes. I wouldn't have painted anything if I had known it would get discussed in this way. I was embarrassed enough as it was that I had put that cross in the hole. Why did they have to talk about it that way?

Doing something is important

I learned something that day about expressing feelings during depression. Writing, or talking, or painting, or whatever it is that grabs us (even Mary's wretched woven baskets too, I suppose) is very, very important. These things can give us ways of expressing ourselves without using words. When feelings are locked up inside us they cramp our style for the climb. *If we can get those feelings out into the open we have much more chance of understanding them and freeing ourself from them.* I discovered that some of those feelings are positive. I had some kind of hope. I hadn't realized that.

We should not let our fear hold us back from pursuing our hopes.

John F. Kennedy

Expressing feelings can be dangerous

I learned too that this externalizing of our feelings can be rather dangerous. What we feel when we are depressed is very personal. It is vital to understand what is going on inside us. However, whoever is shown the feelings must be trustworthy, and able to control their own opinions so that the depressed person feels safe enough to go on exploring those feelings. I thought that I trusted Frank reasonably well, but his dissection of my painting left me distinctly uneasy.

The next week when we did painting again, Annette and I fooled about and painted a huge mural of our worst nightmares outside, and then tried to paint into the picture all the faces of the staff and patients. Word got around and patients came to sit for a portrait.

I painted Frank with a wagon-load of tranquillisers. The previous week when he had finally finished his brush-stroke by brush-stroke analysis of my paintings, I tore them all up and threw them in the bin. He had retorted with such a massive dose of valium that I can remember my room swimming around me before I had a chance to get myself into bed. But I remembered that cross I had painted.

It was to be one of the turning points in my climb out of depression.

Hope has two lovely daughters, anger and courage.

Augustine of Hippo

14

What preparations can I make?
Creativity is the successful resolution of internal conflict.

A psychiatrist

Somehow, however painful or impossible, or however much of a waste of time it seems, I must make the decision to climb up or life will stay this terrible. Of course terrible lethargy and hopelessness will strike! 'What's the point . . .?'

Once we have made the decision to try to climb up out of depression, there are a few things we can do to get ready for the climb. Having been through many phases of depression, I have learned that if I sit around waiting for it all to get better, I will have a very long wait. So we need to make a start with something.

How do we start?

◆ With something small.

◆ With just one thing.

◆ With some kind of 'action plan'.

Although taking some action is essential for our climb up out of depression, the beginning of our action plan needs to be realistic. It's best to sit at the bottom of the cliff, or on some safe ledge, until we feel fit and ready. This is important preparation time. It is a time of making our resolve and planning our ascent.

One step at a time

It's no good moving along on a front—trying to do lots of improving things at the same time. I find that although it seems painfully slow, for me, I must tackle one thing at a time. I never get anywhere when I write in my journal about needing to be more outgoing. Yuk! It's far too general, so enormous and overwhelming, and the thought so terrifying, that I give up before I start. But, if I tell myself that I could manage go out tonight, or I could ring that one person to see how she is, I can cope. That is because these are small and manageable things to do.

▨ Don't worry about the overhang ahead

In climbing, it is important to tackle just one bit at a time—the bit you are on at the moment. It's not that we shouldn't think about the future, as clearly we must plan for some things. But if we worry about the overhang ahead, we will not be concentrating on the bit that needs attention now. If we don't concentrate, we will fall off now.

So when depression strikes, and the thought of the whole day ahead, or what must be done tomorrow or next week, brings total panic, just concentrate on the next ten seconds.

When you have grasped those ten seconds, you may find you can contemplate the next ten minutes. In the bad times I try never to have to think too much beyond the next ten minutes. It sends me into total blind panic. Then when I've done that ten minutes, I tell myself how well I did it. Now I can think about the next ten minutes. Eventually I learn that maybe life is not that bad—today. Maybe I can manage it. So maybe I could think of going to the shop to get some milk.

▨ Doing a little bit every day

Climbing out of depression is like keeping the kitchen tidy, or stopping the house from looking like the store-room of the local charity shop. Doing a little bit every day is the key.

When I am teaching I promise myself to tidy my desk every day before I go home. However bad life gets at work (and it can be devastatingly awful for teachers), those few minutes pay off. If I let myself look around the classroom and think of all there is to do I might be so overcome by it all that I do nothing!

Depression is just like the rest of life in that way—it is so big, so overwhelming, so mysterious, and so irritatingly difficult to get a grip on, that I can easily give up in the attempt. The only way to proceed is to take a little bit of it. When we deal with it in little chunks, we can experience some success. *Succeeding at anything is a terrific antidote to depression!*

It looks worse from down here than it really is

Standing at the foot of the cliff, looking up, gives us a very distorted view of what it is actually like. Every lump looks like a gigantic overhang. The tiny crevices seem far too small to jam a foot or a fist into. The more we look, think and worry about it, the more impossible it seems.

Before we get into a total panic, we need to decide to get the lifeline on, check our helmet is done up, and make a start.

Exercise, creativity and diet

There is a close relationship between the state of the physical body and the state of the mind. We will get better from depression in our mind much more quickly if we also take care of our physical bodies.

Anyone who sits indoors all day, doing very little and eating all sorts of things that are 'bad' for them, is likely to feel depressed.

I have learned, when I notice the tell-tale signs of early depression again, to put myself on a rigid diet, and set out on a gentle but increasingly vigorous programme of exercise. I really do feel better on days when I eat fresh fruit and vegetables and go out for a walk than on days when I sit at home and eat chocolate and go to bed for the afternoon.

That is not to say that sometimes a retreat to bed is not needed. It is. And it is certainly not to say that we should not eat chocolate! (Hell has no chocolate.) But I am saying that a part of our climb out of depression is to get out bodies gradually fitter. This makes us feel better about ourselves. We need to care for our bodies. They are the only ones we have and getting spares is very complicated.

Physical exercise

When we do something that requires physical exercise, we awaken a part of ourselves that otherwise lies dormant. This can develop a feeling of wellbeing.

Apparently, exercise triggers the release of substances called 'endorphines' in the brain, and these cause a sense of wellbeing. I can certainly vouch for the fact that when I do something physical, I feel better. It improves my mood and reduces my anxiety.

It doesn't have to be something violently energetic like swimming or jogging. Just a few stretching exercises in the bedroom, cleaning part of the house, or five minutes dancing to music (with the blinds pulled to stop the neighbours thinking we've finally flipped!) can be enough to lift our spirits. A walk to the shops to get some bread can be the thing that will get us out of the 'slough of despond' some days. The important thing is to find out what works for us, and when.

The trouble is that terrible lethargy strikes. We look at the dust. We think of all the jobs that need doing. We don't know where to start. So we have another cup of tea and decide that we will leave cleaning the windows until we 'feel like it'.

That's just how depression is. It doesn't seem worth cleaning the house. It will just get dirty again. We seem to drift through the day getting little done. We look at the dust again. Maybe tomorrow. But tomorrow will be the same unless we make a start.

Making a start with some exercise

If you are not used to exercise, or if you are over thirty-five, check with your doctor first.

◆ Don't start with anything violent! Start gently and work up very slowly. If you overdo it, you will ache all over, perhaps injure yourself, and give up.

◆ Do gentle warm-up exercise to start with, then remember to do 'cool down' stretches at the end. This stops your muscles from complaining too much.

◆ Choose something that suits your lifestyle and that you could come to enjoy doing. Dancing, brisk walking, swimming and jogging are all things that we can do on our own. Some people get more out of exercise if they join a local gymn, or a tennis club, or do something with a friend.

◆ You need to work up to about twenty minutes of exercise at a time. This may take several weeks. Twenty minutes seems to be enough to get those messages of wellbeing to our brain and to get our hearts doing the things that doctors tell us they should be doing. But if you get out of breath, or feel some pain, stop.

◆ Keep some sort of note of what you do. It really helps a sense of progress. I write down briefly what I have done on a spare calendar, so yesterday's entry read 'swam 20 mins'. If I do this I can see that I am building up strength and stamina, and check that I am doing something about three or four times a week.

◆ Don't exercise if you feel ill, or on days when you suspect you may be sickening for something. It will only make you take three steps backwards.

Doing something creative

Something creative, such as writing, sewing, painting or singing, makes us feel better. All the depressed people I know agree on that.

Doing something—it doesn't matter too much what—is the way to change the decision to climb up into the reality of the first step.

When the physical and the creative come together we can get the great benefit from the combination. Maybe that is why gardening is such a popular hobby. People may not need to grow cabbages and peas to survive. They grow them because they enjoy growing them. It's great fun to buy the packet of seed in the spring, hack away at barren earth, and then experience the joy of seeing the green shoots appear. Gardening makes me feel that God and I are working together on something. That makes me feel good. I do get horribly murderous thoughts about rabbits, pigeons and slugs though. Why do they always eat my baby plants and seem not to touch Ted's next door? This could be evidence of my paranoia—but it's true, the world, and especially the rabbits, are against me!

> **Those who sow in tears
> will reap with songs of joy.**
>
> **The psalmist**

Psychologists and psychiatrists argue about how much body chemistry influences depression. I'm not qualified to comment because I don't understand it. What I do know is that there are some things (medication, diet, exercise and so on) that can influence the way we think.

Herbal teas help me to sleep. Keeping off coffee helps me not to tremble. Chewing sugar-free gum helps me to cope with nausea. Exercise makes me feel good. State of mind and state of body are very closely linked.

There are some things about depression that, for some, will need more than the home remedies I describe in this book. Going into hospital or being a day patient can seem very drastic, but the routine of the day, and having no responsibility (which helps you to concentrate on what it is that is bugging you) can be very calming and reassuring.

Some people get better from depression by being in a hospital Occupational Therapy department, and doing craft work. For other people, being forced to sit there every Tuesday and Thursday morning is a practice for hell.

It's a case of finding out what works for you. Note down in your journal what it was about a day that made it almost tolerable. That way you will find out what things help you to feel a bit better.

Having a good diet

The decision to make a start on the climb must be based on our fitness. Last summer I didn't go out with my friends on one cliff climb because I felt ill. It would have made it tough going and spoiled the rest of the time on that holiday. It's like that for us on the climb up from depression. If we are unfit, we will climb badly. We'll be likely to fall off and that will make us lose our confidence.

Those who have got better from depression recognize the importance of having a good diet. And 'real' food is better than processed or convenience food.

Many experts agree that the features of a good diet are that it is:

low in fat; the fats that are used should be polyunsaturated (such as olive oil or sunflower margarine) rather than animal fats

high in fibre; lots of vegetables, whole grains and cereals, such as wheat, oats and rice

as varied as possible so it includes a full range of vitamins and minerals—things such as muesli and mixed salads are ideal

low in sugar and salt.

The 'goodenough' diet

For most of us, getting a good diet has to be some form of compromise.

◆ Convenience foods give us the extra time that we need to survive depression, motherhood, the rigours of working or the fact that preparing a meal drives us crazy.

◆ Treats (such as chocolate or a take-away meal) make us feel happy and relaxed.

◆ Some 'good' food (such as quality wholemeal bread) is much more expensive than mass-produced equivalents, so sometimes we need to buy just what we can afford.

Our diet just needs to be 'goodenough'.

Activity

⤳ Make an 'action plan'. Keep it realistic!

⤳ Keep a diary of exercise and what you eat.

⤳ The diary can focus us into the times when you are likely to eat 'bad' things.

⤳ A diary gives an overall sense of getting somewhere.

One who recovers from sickness forgets about God.
An Ethiopian proverb

15

Things we need to take

He is a man who is impossible to please because he is never pleased with himself.

Goethe

One of the obvious things about climbing is that you need to be dressed for the job. You would hardly set off wearing a bikini and plastic beach sandals and carrying a suitcase stuffed with your luggage for the week. But some people attempt to get through life ill-equipped and carrying all sorts of unnecessary and unhelpful 'luggage' with them. We will look at some of the things we need to leave behind (chapter 17) but in this chapter we will look at some of the things we need to take with us—the gear.

Getting on the right gear

Climbing gear is always minimal. But that minimum is essential. As with our 'gear' for life, it isn't the quantity that is important, but having the few essential items.

Preparation for climbing is thorough, and it is only when essential items such as belts, harnesses and helmets have been checked, and the lifeline ropes have been carefully anchored, that the leader will go ahead. As a member of the team I have no choice in this. I obey the rules—or I don't climb.

What do we need for the climb? Our 'essential gear' might be:

a willingness to work at change

a refusal to accept society's stigma of 'mental illness'

a good friend, therapist, doctor, minister or some other carer who will listen to us

some medication, if that's what the doctor recommends

an action plan for working on understanding ourselves (for example, working through the activities in this book)

to keep a journal.

Keeping a journal

Even if we hate writing, most of us are self-centred enough to get something out of writing about ourselves. It can be a most effective way to set about understanding the climb ahead. If we keep even the briefest of jottings in our journal, over the months we may see that there are similarities in our experiences.

Here are some examples:

Every time you go to your in-laws you get headaches

Driving up the motorway makes you feel tense

Eating out late makes you unable to sleep

Drinking red wine makes you feel ill

In the winter months you feel more depressed than in the spring and summer

At the anniversary of a death you develop panic attacks

Gardening makes you feel better

Just before your monthly period you are tense and totally unreasonable

The day after exercise is usually a good one.

We need to discover to learn how we tick. Some of things are quite easy to work out. Others are more complex.

Why does that irritating habit she has drive me up the wall?

What is it about that death that leaves me so devastated?

What is it about society's attitude to women that makes me so angry?

What is it about food that makes me pig-out so much?

In our journals we can try to look for common themes. These are things that crop up time after time and are obviously going to be important in our climb out of depression.

Working with a friend

When you find a pattern, try to work out why it is like that. It's not easy, and it may take many weeks to grasp something. It is helpful to find someone with whom we feel we can share some of our insights.

Work towards talking with someone. Maybe join a self-help group. Various organizations run self-help groups or drop-in centres where people can go and just 'be'. Some groups are specific, such as parents at home with babies. Many are run by people who are, or who have been, depressed themselves, for example those run by the Depressives Associated in Britain. (See the resources list at the back for useful addresses.)

Maybe you would get a great deal from doing the activities in this book with someone else who is depressed.

Life is a story

Writing in a journal or talking with others is partly about telling ourselves our story. This is one way to come to terms with our life and begin to get beyond the trap of despair. We begin to open up possiblities of seeing beyond our tight little lives into what could be and what might be. It's something of an adventure to start to take those first steps up out of depression. All adventures are a bit scary.

Adventure is the meeting of dreams and realities.

Activity: the journal

~~> Writing 'Top Secret—Do Not Read' on the cover is asking for trouble!

~~> Dates are important for looking back. There may be some regular pattern in our depressed feelings.

~~> How often you write will be a reflection of your feelings. Sometimes I write in my journal several times a day. Sometimes I add nothing to it for weeks on end.

~~> Sketches, pictures stuck in, newspaper clippings, family photos and so on all help to capture your feelings and the things that you were thinking. (I keep a picture of puffin in mine, because it reminds me of the beauty of God's creation, the freedom of the sea, and how utterly fantastic puffins are.

There was a time when I was so depressed I thought I would die, but when I saw a puffin, I felt, quite suddenly and unexpectedly, that everything would be OK.)

⤳ The main purpose of the journal is to help us to understand ourselves better, to be able to take a firmer grip on the rock face, and therefore to make the rest of the climb much more straightforward and less painful. (Eventually!)

I've got the gear on, now what?

So you have struggled into the various bits of the gear ready for a climb, and you're standing at the foot of the cliff feeling like a trussed turkey and wishing you had gone to the loo before you put it all on. This is when it all really begins. Climbing isn't just about the gear—helmets and ropes and harnesses. There are three other vital ingredients:

◆ your own grit and determination

◆ the rest of the team

◆ a trustworthy leader.

> **Surprise yourself every day with your own courage.**
> **Denholm Elliott, actor**

16

Life is difficult
Seek not abroad, turn back into thyself, for in the inner man dwells the truth.
Augustine of Hippo

Your own grit and determination will, in the end, be one of the main ingredients for the success of the climb. Anyone who has suffered from depression and has survived the experience long enough to try to do something about it—such as reading a book about it, as you are now—has got the makings of a successful climber.

Those who tell us how good they are at things, or those who get easily to the top, or those who seem to sail through life as if it were one long party, do not have true grit and courage.

When I watch the children at school on the climbing frame, it's not the child who goes straight to the top and stands there looking confident who is the one with the courage. It's the little child who has just come to school and who climbs up slowly and nervously, sometimes slipping off. This child may not even get to the top. Perhaps she goes halfway and then turns round and gives the teacher a timorous smile. I see myself in that kind of child. They will get there one day and it will be all the more important because it took time, a few bruises and a great deal of guts.

Climbing is difficult

At the beginning of his book *The Road Less Travelled* Morgan Scott Peck makes the observation that 'life is difficult'. That seems to me to be a realistic starting point from which to view our climb. If we develop a view that somehow life should be calm, easy, delightful and trouble-free at all stages, we are in for a shock!

The climb ahead of everyone is difficult. Even when we are fit, healthy, well off, at peace with ourselves and terribly happy, there are difficulties to be faced.

There are stages in our lives when we cannot get through the day without being scratched, battered and bruised. It's like those bits of a rock-climb where there is nothing to hold on to, no other way up other than putting your hand right into a crevice and making a fist which jams tight, giving you enough of a hold to pull yourself up. You leave rather a lot of yourself behind on the rock face and it is terribly painful. You just have not to think about it. If you want to get up it will be worth it in the end.

Although the world is full of suffering, it is full also of the overcoming of it.

Helen Keller

Lots of life seems to be about blood, sweat and tears. The moments in history that stick in our minds are moments of great triumph, often only accomplished by the shedding of blood, the loss of life, or by someone giving all to achieve something. Michelangelo didn't get that ceiling in the Sistine Chapel done overnight. Human rights for blacks have cost a lot of lives, and no doubt will cost more. Jesus went through agonies on the cross. It seems impossible therefore, even in our very ordinary lives, to doubt that one of the crucial parts of our survival strategy for our climb is being prepared to get hurt or rejected.

Life is difficult. At times very, very difficult. It takes a lot of courage to face it.

It's OK to go backwards

Many times when I am climbing across a rock face, my moves to find a better hold involve going back or sideways. This sideways moving is called 'traversing' by the leader. He isn't just being polite. It really is OK in climbing to come back down a bit, then go sideways. In fact, sometimes that is the best way to climb.

But that's not how society often sees it.

The values of our society

The values of the society in which I live seem to have become very competitive. I don't know enough about history to know how that came about. Some people have told me that competitiveness is 'basic to human nature'. Is it? When I climb I experience something that is about 'success' and about 'getting to the top', but it isn't competitive. It's a team effort, and also about an individual's achievement for its own sake, not measured against any one else's efforts.

So much of society seems to value success in a different way:

◆ the only thing that matters in life is to Get On

◆ your personal value is measured by your degree of success, which in turn is measured by how far up the ladder you have moved (and sometimes by how many people you managed to knock off on the way).

◆ you are measured by the amount of money that you earn.

The education system sometimes gives out the message that the only thing that matters is to pass exams and get into college. Those children who do not 'manage it' often assume they are no good and useless. They do not see their value as human beings. Those who do often feel the need to go on succeeding in everything all through life.

If a child lives with approval, he learns to live with himself.

Dorothy Law Nolte

When I was just a mother at home (note how that word 'just' creeps in), I almost felt I had to justify my existence to some people. For some reason I found this worst at dinner parties. People would peer at me and say, 'And what do you do?' 'I'm a mother,' I would say, and a great silence would follow. I let this develop over the years into 'I'm doing the most important job in the world—raising children.' Not all were convinced.

To be anyone worthwhile I had to be 'someone'—a secretary or a nurse, anything. It is exactly that attitude that works against us building up our self-esteem. Life isn't measured by what we do, but by who we are. That terrible cliché contains another one of those Great Truths. I don't think God gives out points for what jobs we do—5000 for a brain surgeon and three if you screw the tops on tubes of toothpaste. But that's often how we feel valued by society. (You only get one point if you work at home doing the washing up and wiping snotty noses.)

And it is exactly this attitude that we pick up and allow to contribute towards our depression.

Getting a realistic view of what our problem really is

As well as these attitudes from others, those who are depressed often do not value themselves very much. Having a low self-image is very, very common indeed among depressed people. It shows itself in the things that we say, 'I'm useless,' 'I'm ugly,' 'Everything I do fails,' 'I can't do anything about it.'

This affects the way we look after ourselves and the way we dress. What's the point in brushing my hair? Why wear nice clothes? None of that will do any good.

This lack of care for ourselves can mean that we do not eat well, or take exercise, and perhaps that we abuse our bodies with too much medication, alcohol, smoking or other drugs. When all this is linked with the sleep problems of being depressed it is little wonder that we feel so ill!

Man is what he believes.

Anton Chekhov

It's best to climb with others

One of the very best things about rock-climbing is the companionship of others who want to do the same. We all encourage and help one another. No one thinks any less of me when I can't get up a climb. We're all in it together and shared successes (and failures) are things that hold us together as a group and the stuff of hugs and tears.

Not only is it more fun in a group, it is also very much safer. It's just plain stupid to set out on our own. The trouble is that we can feel so alone during depression that we cannot sense companionship that may be there. Loneliness is one of the hardest things to deal with in life.

Sometimes, when things get very bad, we feel we need someone to help us urgently and desperately (and it gets very desperate at times), but we feel unfit to face anyone. ('They won't want to bother with me.') That's low self-esteem. If you knew someone was desperate for help, you wouldn't want them not to ask, would you? Our carers can sometimes be upset by our inability to trust their concern.

It's hard to ask though and the best way to resolve this type of problem may be to join a self-help group. There is a list of organizations you could contact at the end of the book.

Helpers get it wrong

Many of the people who set out to help us inevitably get it all wrong.

◆ They ask us questions ('Are you OK?' 'Do you want a cup of tea?'),
   and we hate that because we cannot make decisions.

- They cook our favourite meal but because at that moment we are off food we burst into tears.

- They tidy the kitchen and we feel threatened because it may be a subtle way of telling us that they wish we would keep the place neater.

- They put fresh flowers in the hall and we cry because they will die there and looked so pretty on the rockery.

- They suggest (in great kindness) that we get a new coat and we think it means we should do something about our dishevelled appearance.

Of course they will get it wrong. Depression is so incomprehensible, individual and isolating that they can hardly do otherwise.

Is the leader reliable enough?

The leader is crucial to the success of any rock-climbing. It matters who you listen to and whom you model your life on. There are lots of 'rules' in climbing which are taught by the leader. They make life easier, keeping your body away from the rock so that you can see what you're doing and giving you better balance. Above all, when you learn to climb, you learn to listen to the leader.

Our leader

The people who we counted as our leaders when we were children (parents, teachers, aunts, grandparents and so on), sometimes expected us to be able to make the climb quite ill-equipped. Indeed, for many of us it felt as if some people were concentrating hard on stamping on our fingers just as we thought we had found a handhold. They seemed not to care about holding the lifeline when we thought they were. They wandered off, just when we needed them, leaving us exposed and in danger.

Some of these people were not good leaders and, when we followed their example, we ended up scrabbling up the cliff using any technique we could think of. We got horribly injured as we did it, and increasingly frantic as we felt ourselves slipping.

If all we have known is this ill-equipped scrabbling at life, our choices are too restricted for us to be able to make rational and sensible life-saving ones.

There isn't actually anything 'good' about being at the bottom of the cliff, but when we are on the flat bits it is a little easier to rest and consider the options. One of these options is to think about some better equipment, to consider who might be a better leader than those we have had so far, and to make some more informed choices—painful and embarrassing though they may be.

And now unto him who is able to keep us from falling and lift us from the dark valley of despair to the bright mountain of hope, from the midnight of desperation to the daybreak of joy; to him be power and authority, for ever and ever.

Martin Luther King

Who shall I choose as a leader?

The people we choose to be our leaders profoundly influence how we climb through life. If we choose to follow and support those who live by putting others down, or by violence, or those who put themselves first, it will be reflected in the way we climb.

If, on the other hand, we choose to be like those who live for others, or those who work for peace and justice in this crazy world, these attitudes will become ours and show in the way we climb.

It matters whom we follow and whom we trust.

Think

~~> What sort of 'worth' do I think people give to me and to what I do? Do I feel that people put me down, or undervalue me?

~~> What sort of 'worth' do I give myself? Do I undervalue myself?

~~> Who are the people whom I respect, or would like to be like? List them.

~~> Who do I trust to be my 'leader'?

My sheep hear my voice and I know them and they follow me.

Jesus in the Gospel of John

More about **low self-esteem** in chapters 24 and 25.

17

Things to leave behind
Climbing has every kind of emotion in it.
Chris Bonnington, climber

There is something wonderfully carefree about my teenagers and their friends. Despite having had me tell them for years to wrap up warm, I notice now that they go out for whole days just in the clothes that they stand up in. No jacket. Nothing for 'just in case'.

Although I'm not the type of person who turns up for a four-hour ramble across the local hills with enough to keep a family of five alive for a week, I was trained in the Girl Guides to 'be prepared'. I learned as a mother to take sticking plaster, tissues and so on just for a trip to the local park. As an attitude to life, though, I'm not sure that mine is a healthy one.

Of course, it is sensible to be prepared. But what about the things that we don't need?

We don't need to go on our climb with a rucksack stuffed full of things we could survive without. We get bogged down and worn out with our burden, and we would be much better without it.

That's where I think my teenagers have got it right with life. They just take themselves, a few friends, and they are off.

79

If I had my life to live over—I'd dare to make more mistakes next time. I'd relax. I would limber up. I would be sillier than I have been this trip. I would take fewer things seriously. I would take more chances. I would take more trips. I would climb more mountains and swim more rivers. I would eat more ice-cream and fewer beans. I would perhaps have more actual troubles, but I'd have fewer imaginary ones.

You see, I'm one of those people who live sensibly and sanely hour after hour, day after day. Oh, I've had my moments, and if I had it to do over again, I'd have more of them. In fact, I'd try to have nothing else. Just moments. One after the other, instead of living so many years ahead of each day.

I've been one of those people who never goes anywhere without a thermometer, a hot water bottle, a raincoat and a parachute. If I had to do it again, I would travel lighter.

If I had my life to live over, I would start barefoot earlier in the spring and stay that way later in the fall. I would go to more dances. I would ride more merry-go-rounds. I would pick more daisies.

Nadine Stair, aged eighty-five

Getting rid of the backpack

In the story of *Pilgrim's Progress* which John Bunyan wrote in prison, Christian sets out on his journey to seek the narrow path to heaven with an enormous and heavy pack on his back. He meets various helpers on the way, and they tell him about a place where he will be able to put his burdens down.

Christian searches for this place, faces many hardships and learns many lessons along the way. One day, to his delight, he feels sure that he is close to the place he is seeking. The path becomes steep and rough and a great struggle to climb, but he is so keen to get rid of his burden that he rushes up it.

At the top of the slope he finds a simple wooden cross. He kneels at the foot of the cross and his burden immediately falls off his back and rolls down the slope, disappearing into an open grave.

Christian stands up and feels the freedom as he is able to

stretch and walk free from the huge load. He stands quietly for a moment, thinking of the person who died on that cross to enable him to walk free: 'He hath given me rest by His sorrow, and life by His death.'

He is so grateful that tears of joy roll down his cheeks as he thinks of that death, and his own freedom. He is so thrilled that he jumps for joy and sings at the top of his voice!

This lovely image of a Christian coming to the foot of the cross and laying down his burden is a good one to meditate on. Most of us do try to get our burdens off and lay them down. We are good at saying 'Oh God, please help me.' The trouble is that we can tend to kneel for a while, then at the end of our thoughts we stand up, and instead of leaving our burdens behind, we pick up the overstuffed backpack again, and trudge off!

Life on the cliff face with a weighty pack on our backs is tough. It is hard to grasp the rock face when all the time we are fearing that we will over-balance and topple off.

How do we learn to put down our burdens?

Work out what they are. It can take some time. These 'burdens' can be many varied things:

Negative self-talk, e.g. 'I'm no good' (see chapter 18)

A lack of understanding of ourselves

A lack of understanding of what depression is

An unrealistic view of what life is actually about

Unresolved conflict in the family or at work

Feeling so much guilt that we cannot function as free individuals

Holding onto bitterness, or letting jealousy find its way too far into our lives, or harbouring angry thoughts about some old enemy.

Getting rid of feelings of jealousy and bitterness towards someone might just improve the quality of our lives.

Work on growing away from them
This isn't an instant thing. Some days we find that we are carrying all our burdens around. Other days we seem to be free of them

for a bit. It is important to be aware of those moments of respite and happy in them. It gives us hope of what life can be like at the top of the climb.

The climb out of depression is helped by cashing in on those moments when we realize the burdens have left us for a while. This morning the dread seemed a little less. The thought of getting up was not one of total terror. Maybe today the sun will shine and I will see the first shoots of spring.

Decide which particular bit of baggage you could wrench from your back first

No one ever got rid of depression by tackling the whole lot in one go. If you cannot face the big things yet (such as forgiving someone for some wrong they did) maybe you can try the easier ones, such as looking at your stress level, or at how you do some things, to see if you make them unnecessarily complex and difficult. For example, if making up lunch boxes for the children to take to school drives you crazy, consider doing them the night before, or (my own method), get the children to do their own.

Maybe it is our tendency towards feeling guilty that makes depressed people great worriers and sometimes over-the-top workers.

> **When I look back on all these worries, I remember the story of the old man who said on his deathbed that he had had a lot of trouble in his life, most of which never happened.**
>
> **Winston Churchill**

The success of the climb depends on on putting down the burdens. This is essential for a successful climb out of depression.

The activities in this book are designed to make it much clearer what the burdens are. When we know what it is that is weighing us down, it is easier to get rid of it.

◆ The bitter old lady who will not let bygones be bygones develops a pointing finger. She is so determined to keep accusing that she loses her ability to grip onto the cliff face.

◆ The jealous man is so preoccupied with what he hasn't got that he fails to appreciate what it is he has got. He loses the ability to feel glad because the sun is shining. He doesn't see the wonder and newness of the beginning of spring.

◆ The angry young woman is so busy shouting her protest that she cannot hear the words of peace she is offered.

◆ The man burdened by guilt fails to recognize the things about life that are meant to be fun and enjoyable. He is so busy worrying about all the guilt that he doesn't appreciate his uniqueness and value.

The silence of God has at all times been a great trial to mankind.
W.R. Inge, Dean of St Paul's cathedral, London

Remember

◆ the activities in this book are not the answer to everything with a promise of eternal bliss just around the corner, they are simply to help you to decide what are the right questions for you to ask about your depression.

◆ If something doesn't prove helpful, abandon it and try something else. If we are also able to ask ourselves why something is unhelpful, we will be a bit wiser and nearer the top of the climb.

If all else fails today, go out and pick daisies, or dance barefoot on the grass, or . . .

Activity

⤳ Review your action plan for getting out of depression (see part 4).

⤳ Make a list of what might be the burdens that you are carrying up the climb.

I feel the capacity to care is the thing which gives life its greatest significance.
Pablo Casals

More about:

negative self-talk, chapter 18; **lack of understanding ourselves**, chapter 19; **lack of understanding what depression is**, chapters 5 and 6; an **unrealistic view of what life is actually about**, chapter 16.

18

Negative thinking

A man cannot possibly be at peace with others until he has learned to be at peace with himself.

Bertrand Russell

What is low self-esteem?

Low self-esteem has many features. It can sometimes be hard to see in some people who project a cheerful and coping self to the world. We come to recognize in ourselves that inside the apparently calm, confident or exuberant individual that we are prepared to let the world see, there may be a terrified person who we think we need to conceal.

If you believe that you are bad and unacceptable you are unable to look back at your past with pleasure and towards your future with hope. Only bad things happened to you in the past and only bad things will happen to you in the future.

Dorothy Rowe

Here are some of the ways we can recognize low self-esteem:

◆ A lack of confidence. 'I can't do that.' 'Everything I do goes wrong.' 'I failed again. I always fail. I'm no good.'

◆ A feeling of guilt that won't go away. 'It's all my fault.'

◆ Feelings of self-hatred. 'I hate myself. I'm useless.'

◆ A poor body image. 'I'm ugly.' 'I'm too fat/thin/tall/short.' 'I don't like the shape of my nose/face/hips.' 'The only hope for me is plastic surgery.'

◆ 'I am a hopeless and useless person.'

At its very worst, people with low self-esteem believe that the world would be a better place if they were dead.

We may eventually come to recognize that it is our low self-esteem that underlies our problem of depression.

Where does low self-esteem come from?

Once the idea of perceiving ourselves as failures and no good gets a hold on us it is a struggle, sometimes a deadly struggle, to get rid of these thoughts. Understanding how we came to think that way can be a great help. Almost certainly we didn't come out of the womb believing that we were useless!

Criticism during childhood

In his book about depression *Roots of Sorrow*, Dr Richard Winter identifies one major cause of low self-esteem as heavy criticism in childhood. He says that those '. . . who think they are useless and a waste of everyone's time, have often been heavily criticised in childhood and told they are hopeless failures. Even if the displeasure is never voiced, they may be nurtured in an atmosphere of "you are not intelligent or beautiful enough for me to be proud of you and accept you". Without the basic need for significance being met, they grow up with an aching void within and a deep longing for approval, acceptance and love.'

The inability to trust

If, during our early years, we learn that it is unwise to trust people, we learn also not to trust ourselves.

In his book *God of Surprises*, Gerard Hughes expresses this beautifully:

The greatest emotional needs in childhood are for protection and affection, for without these the child cannot learn to trust himself or anyone else. The ability to grow humanly is proportionate to our ability to trust.

Without that basic trust in ourselves, it seems that all sorts of irrational beliefs come to rest in our minds as we are cut loose in childhood and forced to find our own way up the climb. These beliefs sit in our minds and result in irrational behaviour and thinking.

The tiny child who is unable to trust those around her, for they do not give her unconditional love, learns to trust no one. Not even herself. Here are the beginnings of a depression.

Misplaced guilt

The irrational beliefs that somehow things are as bad as they are because of something that is our 'fault' can grow from childhood.

It is alarmingly easy for children to be in a situation that they cannot cope with or comprehend, and to come out of it with the firm belief that they caused the problem.

◆ When parents argue, or if they split up, the child assumes it is because she was naughty, or that she is unloved.

◆ The death of someone that a child knows may be perceived as having been his fault.

We become 'blamers'. It takes a while to learn that blaming, especially of the mutual kind—'It's your fault,' 'No, it's your fault,'—is uncreative. Growth comes through accepting responsibility and trying to get beyond 'blame'.

The growth of fear

Things that children cannot understand become the stuff of nightmares and the root of negative thinking.

The death of a grandparent or parent may be perceived by a child as not only something that they somehow caused, but an abandonment that they actually deserved. The idea 'I must be such a bad person,' begins to grow in their mind and by the time they are adolescents this has been translated into 'I am such a bad person that no one will ever love me.'

There may be a fear of being abandoned that permeates every aspect of life. It may show itself in perfectionism. 'If I do it perfectly then they will love me.' It may show itself in exhibitionism. 'No one loves me so I must draw attention to myself over everything.'

Fear that we will be left alone, unloved and uncared for, is a fear that can escalate out of control during depression. It is made worse because we often sleep badly, have nightmares, and because any depression tends to bring with it a sense of total alienation from everyone and everything.

If one of my greatest fears is of not being loved; during depression I will come to believe that that is actually what is happening. That is certainly what it feels like. However much those around us may believe that they are helping and caring, we cannot appreciate it as that because we perceive ourselves to be isolated. In the pit. Cut off from all human contact.

This makes the fear worse. Death seems like a good idea.

Activity

~~→ Write your own obituary.

~~→ Write what people might say about you at your funeral service, or in a short piece in the local paper. Resist the temptation to write about how hopeless you are! Think what good points someone would focus on in a tribute to you.

(This activity is from *God of Surprises* by Gerard Hughes.)

I can pardon everyone's mistakes but my own.
Marcus Porcius Cato (234–149BC)

Negative thinking

One of the things that is common amongst depressed people is that when something happens we say to ourselves, 'It was all my fault,' 'If only she hadn't died . . .' 'I should have done that differently,' 'What if it all goes wrong?' 'She really hates me.'

This is negative thinking and the 'what if's and 'if only's can rule our lives and ruin any effective plans for getting better from depression.

One way to spot if we think in this way (and most people do from time to time) is to note down what we are thinking when something goes wrong or upsets us. It may be that our depression has made this type of negative thinking such a habit and so powerful that it is the thing keeping us depressed.

Sometimes it is hard to identify negative thinking. We have had a lifetime to get it down to a fine art. We need to practise both identifying and changing it. I carried various charts in my pocket and used them to work on my thinking for a few weeks. I was astonished at how much I thought in this negative way and I was surprised to find that I could change it.

I really did! I changed the way that I was thinking!

▨ Activity

This is my own version of one of the most useful activities I ever did to help my depression. It really is worth giving it a go so I would encourage you to try this, even if it sounds stupid.

⤳ 1 Read all the way through this activity.

⤳ 2 Copy the chart opposite.

⤳ 3 Put it in your bag or pocket with a pencil. I found it helpful to have several copies, some at work and some at home.

⤳ 4 How to use it:

Situation. In this box write down what happened or what the event was e.g. cooking dinner, or in a meeting at work.

Automatic thought. In this box write down what the automatic thoughts were. 'I'm no good at cooking.' 'She really hates me.' 'Everything I do goes wrong.' Write down what you are telling yourself about these thoughts. 'That proves I'm no good.'

Rational response. Try to make some rational response and challenge the automatic thoughts. Sometimes we can do that straight away. Sometimes it used to take me several days. We get quicker.

Emotions. Give percentages to your feelings/emotions at the time of the incident, e.g. upset 100%, guilty 60%, anxious 100%.

The boxes underneath are for later—either that day or, when you first set out trying to do this activity, it might be very much later. The idea is that we learn to see that what we think at the time something happens is not quite what we may think when we feel calmer.

Corrected thoughts. 'Just because I burned that pie it doesn't mean I will never make a decent meal.' 'Just because they didn't ring me doesn't mean they dislike me.' 'Just because she criticizes me doesn't mean that I am hopeless at my job.'

Any outcomes. You can reflect on how you dealt with the difficult situation. You can see what you have learned. You can try to make it (a) more positive (b) more balanced (c) fit the evidence. We learn to look for other explanations. 'Maybe he ignored me because he didn't see me.'

Date:	Situation or Event:	
	What was I doing/thinking? What happened?	

Automatic thoughts:	Rational Response:	Emotions:
in the situation. How much do I believe them? (0–100%)	What did I think when it happened? What responses to these thoughts can I make?	then. How much do I believe them? (0–100%)

L A T E R   R E S P O N S E S

Corrected thoughts:	Any outcomes?	Feeling/Emotion:
and how much do I believe them? (0–100%)	What have I learned about people/myself? What can I do now?	later. How much do I believe them now? (0–100%)

Feeling/emotion later. We can monitor our feelings. For example, a day later all the guilt may have gone (so the guilt may have been 100%, later it may only be 10%). Maybe we feel some anger. (Maybe even a considerable amount of anger!)

The important thing that I learned from doing these charts was that if I go through the day saying 'if only it was different,' 'that proves that I'm no good,' and so on, then I will feel depressed. It would be hard to feel otherwise!

Playing old familiar tapes

The things that we habitually tell ourselves are the 'old tapes' that we play to ourselves. They have resulted from things that happened to us years ago. These relics of the past may stem from childhood when we had just a child's limited view of the world. We got things wrong then—inevitably.

So maybe we perceived ourselves as useless, unloved, not valued. A child, unable to understand the world around her, concludes that adults are 'good' and 'right' because that is what children are taught to think. Therefore, if an adult treats the child badly, puts her down, or is constantly criticizing her, the child assumes it is she who is 'bad'. These views of ourselves and the world go on playing over and over again in our minds. They become a part of our innermost being.

We tell ourselves we are no good. This is an old tape. It is the beginning of low self-esteem and a common root cause of finding ourselves at the bottom of the cliff.

We need to—and we can—change those 'old tapes' for new ones that are more real and more positive.

Emotions change slowly

A surprising but crucial thing to grasp in doing this is that we can be very logical about something, we can understand it, we can even change our beliefs, ('I'm not useless, I'm an OK person,') but our emotions tell us differently. Emotions change slowly. When our mind tells us it's OK our emotions yell out, 'No it isn't'.

We need to go on working at those 'old tapes' until our emotions follow. That's hard work.

Come to me, all you who are weary and burdened, and I will give you rest. Take my yoke upon you and learn from me, for I am gentle and humble in heart, and you will find rest for your souls. For my yoke is easy and my burden is light.

Jesus in Matthew's Gospel

What am I saying to myself?

Our self-esteem and our ability to love ourselves and others in the right way rests on the fact that God loves us. Each person is unique and infinitely valuable to him.

Dr Richard Winter

One of the most useful things that I have learned to do in the last few years is to identify what it is that I am telling myself. Most of us have this 'negative self-talk'.

This way of dealing with our problems (identifying our negative thinking) is the basis of 'cognitive therapy'.

As we go about our ordinary lives, these 'old tapes', stuck in our minds and repeatedly blaring out at us, tell us such things such as:

> **'I'll always fail at everything that I do.'**
>
> **'Everything is against me.'**
>
> **'I'm always...'**
>
> **'Because...happened to me when I was five, I can never get away from it.'**
>
> **'I am utterly alone now and always will be.'**
>
> **'God doesn't love me.'**
>
> **'No one loves me.'**
>
> **'I am of no value.'**

These 'old tapes' are, for many of us, one of the root causes of our depression.

OK, your hormones got out of balance at the birth of the baby. Yes, the death was hard to cope with and was the trigger for it all.

Yes, the menopause is hell. Yes, being unemployed is terrible. Yes, looking after dad for all those years drove you crazy.

But it is the old tapes from long ago and from those recent horrendous experiences that keep the icy fingers of depression around our innermost being. Crucial to our successful climb out of depression is the identification of what is on these old tapes— our negative self-talk.

The ten commandments of self-defeat

Some years ago a friend in America showed me these 'ten commandments'. They were written by Richard L. Mason. They are funny, but sum up the most profound and difficult-to-identify beliefs that we have about ourselves and about our world.

And the devil saith unto his angels, 'Wreak havoc on the earth. Create unhappiness everywhere. Sow fear, worry, anger and depression in Jerusalem, in Judea and to the uttermost parts of the earth. For as I go, so send I you.'

And one of the angels, whose name was Blame, settled on the fertile valleys along the Ohio river. There he began to teach the ten commandments:

1. Thou shalt never make mistakes.

2. Thou shalt upset thyself when things go wrong.

3. Thou shalt blame thy neighbour as thyself.

4. Thou shalt neither love, nor forgive, nor accept thyself.

5. Thou shalt always expect things to be different from the way they are.

6. Thou shalt seek the love and approval of everyone for everything that thou doest.

7. Thou shalt avoid facing life's difficulties, remembering that thou canst not change because thou art trapped by thy past.

8. Thou shalt be preoccupied with whatever bothers thee.

9. Thou shalt wait passively for happiness to come unto thee.

10. Thou shalt be dependent mostly on others for thy happiness.

And as Blame taught the people of the valleys, they believed him. In great numbers they came, and heard and

believed, so that the earth was truly filled with fear, worry, anger and depression.

Think

~~> Read through the 'ten commandments' slowly and carefully. Jot down things that come to mind. Try to talk to someone about the things you are thinking.

Activity

~~> Go on with using the negative thinking chart. If you are finding it hard to get going, try to identify just one negative thought on the first day.

When we are used to the chart the sorts of things that we find out about our way of thinking about ourselves might be:

'I'm no good. I do everything wrong.' When a situation starts to go wrong we blame ourselves automatically.

'They hate me,' 'No one appreciates me,' 'Our marriage is falling apart.' When someone fails to give us the affirmation we thought we needed and deserved ('What a totally wonderful pie that was').

'I might just as well be dead.' When we feel we cannot possibly get up and go to work. It proves that we are useless, that life will always be this bad.

Why did that hurt so much?

Further use can be make of the negative thinking chart when we have used it a few times. We can start to 'challenge' or analyze our thinking. (This idea is from David Burns' book *Feeling Good—the New Mood Therapy*.)

Beware! Doing this activity can be fairly terrible! I've written out one example from one of my charts a few years ago and the note at the end of it says 'this was hell to write'. It was such hell that I remember vividly, even now, the trauma of trying to work through it.

Do this on a day when you are feeling strong!

1 Take one negative thought from a negative thinking chart you have done. For example, on one of my charts that I did after a meeting in which my boss repeatedly criticized me in front of my colleagues, I wrote 'she (my boss) really hates me'.

2 Try to work out why that negative thought from the 'old tapes' hurt so much. I did this in a series of questions and answers, trying to answer the negative thought with a positive answer.

3 Go on doing this until you can get to a basic underlying belief that you have about yourself.

These basic underlying beliefs that we have about ourselves are important because they can include the things that are keeping us depressed. We need to find out what they are.

Getting someone else to help you to answer your negative thoughts with positive ones might be helpful.

Negative automatic thought: 'She really hates me.'

Positve answer: 'So what? Other people love me.'

I noted in my journal that my self-esteem, my worth as a person, was very bound up with other people valuing me. I had this underlying belief that I was only worthwhile if other people thought so. This was made much worse in a professional situation in which I was continually criticized. The exercise didn't make the criticism any easier to cope with, but I learned something about myself and about why I was finding it so stressful.

The exercise worked with most negative thoughts, some more easily than others. For some, however, I needed someone to work with me.

As I worked with these charts over the next few months another thing became clear. I only saw myself as a worthwhile person when I was working in a paid job. This explained a great deal about my lifestyle and about my view of myself.

Getting to these underlying beliefs about ourselves is a crucial survival strategy for living.

If you believe that you are bad and unacceptable you see your anger as evidence of your badness. Thus you cannot cope with your anger or anyone else's anger.

Dorothy Rowe

PART 5

HANGING ON

19

Getting to know ourselves

It is only when we possess ourselves that we can give ourselves to others, [but] if what we possess feels wrong, bad, or wicked, then we not only try to hide it from others, but we also try to hide it from ourselves.

Jack Dominian

If we are ever to hang on and climb up out of depression, one of the vital things we need to do is to get to know ourselves. We need to know our strengths and weaknesses, and what, inside us, makes us as we are.

We need to know how to pace our lives. If you're like me, you will have good days and bad days. Sometimes the bad days go on for weeks and months, but you *will* get more done on some days than on others.

On good days I know I can get lots of things done. I just have to be careful not to do too much, although it is tempting, because then I get exhausted. I try to make myself stop well before bedtime, take a shower and then relax.

If you have ever been given the label 'manic depressive' (one of my own collection), then this pattern of overdoing it some days will be familiar to you. It's difficult to develop the skill for both 'making hay while the sun shines' and yet not leaving yourself shattered for the next day.

It's all a question of pacing yourself. To do that well you need to get to know what makes you tick.

I suppose that being kind to ourselves we might be in danger of turning into the most terrible procrastinators, but I think that this is a danger we need to learn to live with.

Surviving the climb out of depression is not just one long (desperately long) climb. It goes in fits and starts. Quite a lot of stops too.

Sometimes we need to retreat

Giving up today and retreating somewhere safe is not a 'bad' thing to do. It is nothing to feel guilty about. Depressed people seem to suffer most dreadfully from guilt. Most of this guilt is totally inappropriate. We need to see it for what it is. It is making us worse!

Giving up today might in the end be a productive and positive thing to do.

'Human becomings'

It is an extraordinarily difficult thing to get to know ourselves. I don't suppose that we ever totally achieve it. It will always be an ongoing process. As someone put it, we are 'human becomings'. We seem, like it or not, to be on a journey. It is an excruciating journey at times and we often feel like throwing in the towel.

I have come to see life as a kind of pilgrimage. I'm very suspicious of those people who give out the message that they have 'got there'. They have arrived. My life never seems to be like that. The minute I think I might have arrived, some other great crisis looms and I realize I haven't. So now I just treat the whole of life as a journey.

'It will be better when . . .'

It is a great mistake to think that the problems that we are facing at the moment will one day go away and that life will be bliss from then on. Our present problems will one day go away, but will be replaced by others. (Hopefully not quite as dreadful as depression!) That's just how life is.

The eighteen-year-old thinks life really begins when he leaves school. The young pregnant woman thinks that all will be well when she's reached her delivery date. The professional thinks that life will get better when she gets that promotion.

'It will be better when we get our new house . . .' 'when I've got more money . . .' 'when the old dear dies . . .' 'when we get married . . .' 'when the kids have left home . . .' 'when . . .'

Of course some things would substantially change our lives for the better. The number of homeless people in Britain and America at the moment is devastating. Today on the news I heard that a volcano in the Philippines erupted—thousands are homeless and many are dead. There are some things that could make the lives of these people so much better that, as someone who has never been homeless, I can hardly understand.

It would be wrong to think that if a homeless family from the streets of my city were given a home tonight (and I wish they were), that all their problems would be over. Some of the very painful and immediate ones obviously would, but, as the days went by, these problems might well be replaced as others took over. The children will get sick, gran will die, and the much longed-for new baby might never arrive.

We often perpetuate a very odd view of real life as something that is trouble free, rather jolly and loads of fun. I don't know anyone for whom life is like that—at least not for long. Life is hard.

There are times when the rich people I know seem to get bogged down by their money and worry so much about it that it seems better to be a bit short of cash! People who get to the top seem to have a life of stress. Those who want promotion will not be satisfied until they get it.

People who have no kids wish they did. Many of those who do have kids worry themselves sick about them. Married people develop a curious intolerance of their spouse. The number of divorces and separations amongst the people I know is alarmingly high. Some single people grieve and are lonely.

Everyone, just everyone, faces problems of one kind or another and when one goes away, another replaces it. Life is like that. When we pat our children's heads and cuddle them saying, 'It'll be all right,' perhaps we should balance out that proper need for reassurance with some explanations of the realities of life.

Maybe we do our children no good thing by only telling them that life is 'all right'? I'm not sure. The truth is that a great deal of the time it isn't all right. At least, it doesn't *feel* all right. But perhaps the world of the child needs to be a world of happy endings and reassurance. Certainly it cannot be right deliberately to give children a tough time because they need to learn that the world is a hard place.

Maybe what we need to do, and teach children to do, is to find a way not of pretending life is free from problems, but of dealing with the problems creatively.

⤳ Do I expect too much of myself?

⤳ Do I have unrealistic expectations of life?

20

Emotions are OK
Through violence you may murder the hater, but you do not murder the hate.
Martin Luther King

Emotions are OK. A bit scary at times, but they are OK. I don't see how they could ever be 'wrong'. They are a part of us. Part of that bit of me that I call my 'heart and soul'. They are a part of the innermost and most vital part of our human-ness. They are how I tell myself what I am thinking and feeling. They are unique and valuable.

Little-understood urges and emotions, pushed under the carpet and out of view, are still there. And if we refuse to acknowledge them they become like a deadly unseen virus in our bodies. Gradually they eat their way into our bodies, our minds and then into our innermost being. Our whole existence will be poisoned unless we pull them out into the open and make some effort to deal with them.

We may feel it would be harmful to let those emotions out, but I believe that it is just as harmful to bury them. In fact it is probably much *more* harmful. Buried emotions come out somehow. And when they do they affect us very deeply.

They can be devastating (we just have to look at the effects of our depression to see that). They are depressing because we cannot understand them, so they make us feel even less in control of our lives than we were. They make us afraid because we cannot understand them. For some of us this could be the root of panic attacks. We are actually afraid of ourselves.

They are frequently inappropriate as they force their way to the surface. So, we may experience furious rage when our child or partner does some small thing. The rage isn't about that small thing. The rage is about something quite different: a buried emotion lurking inside us.

Accepting what I'm really feeling

Accepting that I am angry may be one of the first steps in climbing out of depression. Accepting that I am hurt and damaged may be the first step in working out why I am so depressed. Accepting myself as a sexual being may be the first stage in reaching beyond my guilt to a place where I can say, with great joy, 'thank you God for giving me these wonderful feelings'.

To say that feelings such as anger and sexual urges aren't there is both stupid and dangerous. But admitting they are there is also a dangerous thing. We all know the kind of person who projects a calm persona, but just under the surface is a boiling and murderous rage.

◆ It's dangerous to admit to feelings.

◆ It makes us vulnerable.

◆ It gets close to disclosing that innermost bit of us that is us, our 'heart and soul'.

Getting 'in touch' with our emotions

We go to great pains to protect and conceal the 'unacceptable' part of ourselves which generates strong feelings. We hide it. For those of us who feel the abyss of depression, this hell-hole is our defence against the even worse horrors of our true feelings, buried deep in our innermost selves.

One day, all the pent-up emotion will come bursting through the calm exterior like the steam in a boiler. If its exit is blocked up we will simply explode in a world-shattering and cataclysmic moment of destruction. That's what depression is—our attempt

100

to contain that enormous driving energy boiling and churning around inside us.

The trouble with our buried emotions is that they pop out at us when we are not expecting them. At best this is utterly disconcerting and at worst it can wreck our lives. We do hateful things to those who love us. We cry when it is most inconvenient. We feel destructive anger when a shrug of exasperation would have been more appropriate.

The way out of this trap is to try to feel what we are feeling *at the time*. That's dangerous—and it hurts.

What can I do to get in touch?

Surprisingly, just by doing something creative or active, we can begin to identify what it is that we are feeling—anger, sadness, terror and so on.

Punching a cushion when we feel depressed can help us start to see what may be making us depressed. As we punch, so things come to mind. As we write in our journal we begin to understand ourselves more—we hear what we are thinking. As we create a new windowbox for the spring flowers we hear some of our sadness at the thoughts of the death of the winter.

So, as we begin to piece together our own story of why we are depressed, our feelings become clearer.

Maybe the way the woman in the supermarket treated us yesterday made us feel put down. The hassle with the man who came to service the boiler and left it leaking gas really got to us. The worry about a teenager, an elderly parent, the job we lost, facing up to a death—they can all make us angry, or fearful, or aggressive.

Once we recognize what it is that we are feeling, there is some relief, but also fear.

What now?

Rather like standing at the bottom of a long and difficult climb, beginning to see the extent of those buried feelings is utterly daunting. If we say, 'Yes, I do feel angry/abandoned/unloved . . .' we have no idea where it will end. It is a great unknown. It is the stuff of nightmares.

But to recognize a feeling that we did not know we had is one of our greatest achievements. We begin to get a clearer picture of what is behind our depression. Although this picture is the stuff of nightmares, it is also the very thing that we need in order to make some real difference to our lives—to help us hang on.

Why do I feel this way?

'Why did I get so angry when she said that?' 'Why did I feel such murderous rage at such an apparently small incident?' 'Why has that death left me so fearful three years later?' 'Why?'

It is neither easy nor comfortable to answer these questions, but at least if I know that I am feeling *something*, I am on the first ledge of the climb—it puts me in touch with myself as a person.

When we know we feel something, we know we are at the start of the climb. We are one stage on from the very depths of depression, when things are so bad that we feel nothing.

At the foot of the cliff there is a kind of alienating numbness to life that wraps us in a silent cotton-wool world, because to feel those things that put us there would be too painful. So we feel almost nothing.

Once we begin to feel the rage, or the devastation of having been abandoned, or the horror of believing that it would be better for everyone if we were dead . . . Then and only then do we know we are getting in touch with those feelings, and we are on the first ledge up the climb. We have made a start on the long and difficult climb to understanding ourselves.

That is definitely a Good Thing! But it is also very painful and requires our hard work to deal with it.

> Anyone who feels that they're in some way plugged in to a meaningful, cosmic system is given a greater psychological balance and stability as a result—whether or not they believe it contains a God-like figure at the control panels. And lots of people have this beneficial sense of being plugged in to something bigger, even if they're not religious in the going-to-church-regularly sense.
>
> **Robin Skynner, psychiatrist**

More about **being kind to ourselves**, chapter 7; **anger**, chapter 22; **guilt**, chapter 23.

The following three chapters deal with **fear**, **anger** and **guilt**.

21

Overcoming fear, worry and panic
Excessive fear is always powerless.
Aeschylus, Greek playwright (468BC)

Depression is often accompanied by a devastating fear. If we are going to be able to hang on in our struggle up the cliff face, we need to learn some strategies for dealing with this fear.

It is not like the fear of getting cancer, or of dying in a terrible road accident, or that our baby will die so we have to check every five minutes that she is still breathing. The fear during depression is something else as well.

We can never adequately explain it. It is worse for some than others. It goes beyond total blind panic, or the fear of imminent tragedy. It haunts our lives. It rarely goes away. It makes us feel that at each moment of our day we must fight for our very survival.

This fight for survival can be so terrible that sometimes we give up, and death seems to be a rather inviting option. At least we would get away from the fear.

Facing the fear

It is not always associated with a panic attack—when the heart pounds, we break out into a sweat, we think we may throw up, and there are a thousand angry elephants stampeding through our stomach. The fear is something that just stays in our minds. At the dead of night, when we wake, it is there, lurking, reminding us that we have almost given up hope of ever feeling any different.

It is like walking on a cliff in the dark with a precipice nearby. Any minute now we will plunge to our death.

Sometimes it is worse than others. Maybe these times give us a hint of what lies behind the fear. This is the sort of information we need to note down. When do I feel the fear the most? What does it link with?

For me, the fear seemed to be there all of the time. Then I began to see how it was linked with a quite irrational fear of talking to a therapist about my childhood. There were certain things that would make the fear unbearable—as if life and the universe as I know it would all come to some cataclysmic end.

This gave me some clues, but I had a very effective mechanism that would shut off my thoughts whenever I tried to think what the fear was actually about. I would get some thoughts, the fear would leap out at me, then I would pull down the blind on those thoughts and I could go no further. For months nothing could get me beyond that point.

Clearly it was sensible to leave the blinds down—to raise them would be to cause the end of the world! But I had to get beyond that eventually and learn to acknowledge my fear so that I could do something about overcoming it.

The trap

The fear can easily become horribly entangled with guilt, and we get the feeling that this depression was deserved. It is God punishing us. We are such terrible people that it is only just and right that we should be dealt with in this way.

We both fear death, and long for it to get us away from the fear of this terrible life. It is obvious that, given the strength of our feeling, we contemplate suicide. But what if death brings something much worse than this awful existence? Maybe there is no way forward. Both death and life are equally intolerable. And so the depression tightens its grip on us.

Hopelessness sets in. We start to believe that there is no way out of this trap.

> I have of late—but wherefore I know not—lost all my mirth, foregone all custom of exercises; and indeed it goes so heavily with my disposition that this goodly frame, the earth, seems to me a sterile promontory.
>
> **Shakespeare,** Hamlet

Decisions

This fear can bring a complete inability to make decisions. Do I want an egg or a cheese sandwich? Shall I wear the blue sweater or the green one? (It is no wonder, given this inability to decide these simple things, that our families give up on us.)

There are probably many reasons for this inability to decide, but one is that the fear gives me a lack of belief in myself. Any decision I make is bound to be wrong because I'm so hopeless. I'm going to retreat under my quilt so that I will not have to make any decisions. All I need to do there is hide and survive long enough for the worst of it to pass.

The trouble with that is that others want to help, so they ask, 'What can I do?' 'Would you like a cup of tea?' 'Shall I switch the television on?' All these questions require a decision! I don't know what to say. I'm terrified. If I decide anything some terrible, terrible event will happen to change my life for ever.

The whole universe will explode.

How do we survive the fear?

One way is to look back at our strategies for facing the really bad times (see chapter 12). They can remind us that it will not always be like this. The worst of the fear will pass. OK, it does not go away completely, but at times it gets a little better. Better enough to come out from under the quilt.

An even simpler way to survive is to take a tranquillizer. I'm trying not to do that very much these days, and when I do I use substitutes for the hard stuff that doctors prescribe (which can be addictive) from health food shops. These are mild herbal tranquillizers, usually based on valerian, which are not addictive. I find them very effective and there is never a sense that you must have one in order to survive the next ten minutes as there is with some prescribed drugs. As a short-term relief for the bad times, it seems sensible to me to use what is available. Probably valerian is less harmful than our bodies living in such a state of panic that adrenalin is being pumped out into our blood stream for most of our waking hours, and our heart is beating overtime.

Herbal teas help too. I like the taste, they are soothing, and I have to do something in order to drink them. Sometimes just putting the kettle on can help me back into the ordinary world where maybe there are not too many monsters out to destroy me.

Relaxation exercises are great. They change the rate at which the elephants gallop through my gut. The trouble with these relaxation exercises is that although they are simple, they do require some drive, concentration, and determination to quell the fear by ourselves. That can require a belief in ourselves that we don't always have.

In the end, the fear will pass—a bit—but to get rid of it on a long-term basis we need to understand it. Somehow (usually with the help of some trusted friend or therapist), we must take the fear apart, bit by bit, and look at it long enough to understand it.

It is a long process. I learned not to rush it! It needs time.

Overcoming worry: the death-bed test

We worry terribly about things. But worrying never solved anything or made it better—only worse. When we come up against the overhang on the cliff and it seems an impossibility for life to go on, the death-bed test is good.

We can ask ourselves, will I worry about this on my death-bed?

Our immediate answer is to say, 'Yes'.

But if we think about it, we may find that the thing causing us so much stress will not be something we even remember at the end of our lives.

Some of the things we worry about now will, I suppose, be of great and lasting significance. But when we know that our end is near, what will we be thinking about? Probably not today's major hurdle.

I've used the deathbed test so much that I know it works. I've even developed it to, 'Will I worry about this tomorrow?' Sometimes, on recognizing that the great worry of today will be tiny tomorrow, I can even let it go today. Now.

This has been my most important achievement in hanging on in recent years. Because I was able to change how I think about my worries I have hope that things can change.

Dealing with the worries of today

◆ Keep busy

◆ Make a list of things that need to be done

◆ Set a time limit on worrying. This sounds incredibly stupid, but it works! I decide how long I will allow myself to worry about something. Ten minutes, perhaps, over a cup of tea. When the time is up I make myself go and do something that will get the worry back where it belongs—write a letter, make a phone call or write down what it is that is getting to me. Then I make myself do something else.

◆ Give it the death-bed test.

Dealing with panic attacks

Our bodies go through such a lot when the adrenalin pumps round, telling us that it is all too much.

◆ Develop some way to turn all that stress into action. Punch a cushion, rip the phone directory in half (the old one). This needs to be planned ahead, otherwise you tend to get carried away, which gets expensive and dangerous for those around.

◆ Have some technique for relaxing during a panic attack. Make yourself do it when the panic strikes!

◆ This is rather like the relaxation exercise in chapter 10, but it can be done in a crowd.

   1 **Breathe deeply**

   2 **Tense muscles (not easy to do with people around, but do as much as possible, such as clench fists and tighten foot and leg muscles)**

   3 **Consciously relax every muscle**

   4 **Keep breathing deeply, stay relaxed and face the cause of the panic head on.**

◆ When there is no clue as to why the panic came, try to work out what was going on. Why did the panic come now? What is it that I am so afraid of? (I get surprising answers.)

◆ If strategies for dealing with panic aren't working at the moment, or if life is so terrible that taking the easiest way out is the only way out, then reach for the valerian! That's only a short-term solution, but it's OK for now.

▨ Activity

⤳ 1 Note down what the fear feels like.

⤳ 2 When does it get worse? (It may take several weeks to get a clear picture of what might be the root of the fear.)

⤳ 3 What might the fear be about? (Make a guess. Sometimes our intuitive guesses can give us a clue. It doesn't matter if we are wrong at this early stage.)

One cloud is enough to eclipse all the sun.
Thomas Fuller

22

Understanding our anger
It is easy to fly into a passion—anybody can do that—but to be angry with the right person to the right extent and at the right time and with the right object and in the right way—that is not easy, and it is not everyone who can do it.
Aristotle

108

Getting angry is natural. It's like getting tired, or hungry, or wanting sex. Not a lot we can do about the basic emotion. It's how we handle it and deal with it that we can control. There is not a lot of point in feeling guilty about these basic emotions, especially as we seem to have so little control over them.

Coming to terms with our feelings of hurt and anger is an important part of learning to hang on during the climb. This is especially true if part of our depression is trying to hold down our anger.

Once we begin to see what it is that we are really feeling, and what it is that is behind our depression, we are on the way up the climb.

I often scream and rage at God. I think if he is all omni-whatsit and powerful—like I learned in religious studies at school—then he can handle a temper tantrum from one person. I don't believe he is thinking, 'Good grief, that Sue is a pain in the neck.' I think he is much more likely to be thinking that it is a Good Thing that I am at last recognizing the amount of anger that there is inside me that has been sitting there undealt with for so many years.

You have a right to be angry, but you mustn't turn the anger in on yourself because that only compounds the damage which has already been done. You must turn the anger outwards.

Susan Howatch

If God knows everything about me, he knows that I was thinking angry things anyway. Better to have it out. If I am unimpressed by the way he seems to be organizing life, I tell him with a disapproving roar. When we watch the news on the television and see babies dying for lack of food I think it is understandable that we question God's general management of the universe.

We don't get much explanation about drought, famine, volcanic explosion, hurricane and tidal wave. God can hardly be surprised that we get a little irritated at times, and sometimes raise a clenched fist heavenward. I rather think that he might appreciate our honesty.

Of course, we get angry with *people* too. That's not quite so easy to deal with and not nearly as easy for me to write about!

Am I angry?

Often, the problem with anger is that we do not realize it is there. None of us likes the idea that we might be angry inside. It's very frightening, especially if the anger is so great that it might include murderous thoughts. People have told me that it is as bad to think murderous thoughts as to actually commit murder. Something tells me that that cannot possibly be true. For one you have a dead body and the other you don't. Quite different—especially for the potential corpse.

Controlled expressions of anger

I believe in controlled expression of emotions because part of the reason for depression may be this submerged anger (or any other emotion). When I teach small children at school (quite the most challenging job in the whole universe), I encourage them to pound the big cushions in the reading corner, and to tell me what it is that has made them angry. I reassure them that it is OK to feel that anger—but not such a good idea to go and punch Harry! Maybe they want to go and run around the playground to work off that aggression?

> **Usually when people are sad, they don't do anything. They just cry over their condition. But when they get angry, they bring about a change.**
>
> **Malcolm X**

I'm quite sure that there is no easy answer to understanding and getting rid of buried anger. But what has worked for me is to try to express the anger in ways that don't hurt anyone. These are ways I have found effective:

Kicking a wall. (I once did it to a plasterboard wall and my foot went right through! Check first.)

Making bread. All that punching and kneading the dough is so therapeutic

Furiously digging the garden

Playing some aggressive sport

Going a long way away from everyone, and screaming

110

Running down the street

Punching a big cushion—repeatedly and very hard

Dancing to very loud music.

When I write a letter to God in my journal, I definitely feel better. I'm sure if I didn't do that the anger would be directed at my partner or my children, or at myself in some destructive act. I'm sure God can handle it and I think that level of honesty with him is something to feel glad about.

▨ Think

⤳ Find a quiet corner and start a list of the things that make you angry. What were the things that made you angry as a child? What is it that you still resent and feel bitter about? Your list might read something like this:

I hated it the way my dad was always too busy to play with me.

My mother always nagged me. She made me wear hideous clothes and the other kids laughed at me.

They both wanted me to achieve above anything else. I never felt I was good enough for them. If I didn't get straight 'A's I had failed them.

They favoured my brother more than me.

I hated school.

⤳ List the memories of childhood that still stand out for you. What is the earliest thing you can remember? What is the most frightening thing you have ever experienced? What makes you angry now?

⤳ It is often said that depression is internalized anger. How could you get to find out what anger there may be inside you? You may decide to: ask a trusted friend if they think you are angry inside; keep a note of what makes you feel angry/ anxious/depressed; keep a dream journal; assume that there is anger there, even though you cannot see it, and take up some violent sport such as squash or racquetball, or garden

111

furiously for twenty minutes, or scream at the moon and see if that makes any difference.

➝ Anger may also be revealed through creativity. What could you do to be creative?

read a story

draw or paint a scene from your childhood

join an evening class in pottery

paint a mural on the loo wall

grow cabbages

arrange some flowers in your favourite vase

write a long-overdue letter.

We don't have to stay trapped by what has gone before. We can decide to break free. No one need feel that their life is out of their control. It isn't. Have a good scream at God—he can take it!

23

Managing guilt
Guilt always hurries towards its complement, punishment: only there does its satisfaction lie.
Lawrence Durrell

There is a strong belief in Western society that there is a great deal to feel guilty about. If we have really wronged someone then we should feel guilty. It prompts us to do something about apologizing and trying to put things right. But guilt seems also to surround the basic human emotions that everyone feels.

112

To have guilt about our sexual feelings or our anger seems about as logical as having guilt about being thirsty. It's human to have strong sexual feelings, and to feel furious rage, and it's OK to to be human.

We can 'feel' guilty without being guilty—and we can be guilty without feeling it.

It's not wrong to feel angry, but it is wrong to kick the dog, or murder the person we feel angry with. It's not wrong to feel very sexually turned on but it is wrong to rush out and leap into bed with the first person we meet. It's not the emotion that is wrong, it's how we deal with that emotion.

The kind of teaching that I received as a child and teenager seemed to produce guilt in large doses. For many of us the guilt and frustration and the sheer ignorance of our human urges has left us emotionaly paralyzed. Perhaps this is why so many of us try to bury our feelings. If they are submerged and we cannot see them, we argue that we can control them. But that is not so.

Burying our true guilt so that we cannot see it is a bit like trying to bury an angry lion in a child's sandpit. We can't bury it deep enough to get rid of it. It is potentially a source of harm. The guilt will burst through as depression, or rage or violence. It would have been simpler to deal with the guilt as guilt by apologizing and asking for forgiveness, agonizingly difficult though that is.

False guilt is best got rid of by recognizing that it is misplaced. I'm sure that zealous parents and teachers have got a lot to answer for—me included!

The depressed person can be guilty because she feels she is expected to be some kind of superhuman being.

This guilt and the failure to live up to our own high standards can kill.

This morning our local paper printed a heartrending story of a woman who killed her two children, and then herself. As the whole village met in the church to light candles and pray, they wept without exception as they mourned for this woman whom they described as a perfect mother with delightful children.

The story goes on, becoming more and more inexplicable with reports on the loving husband, the busy community life of the family and the respect that they had in the village. Then at the end there are a few giveaway lines as her father-in-law explains that she had been depressed lately and felt she had failed as a mother.

Guilt is deadly stuff. True guilt can be removed through acknowledgment and forgiveness. False guilt needs to be shown up for what it is.

Prayer is not asking. It is a longing of the soul.
Mahatma Ghandhi

24

Understanding how we see ourselves: our self-esteem
The recurring theme predisposing [people] to depression is rejection and lack of self-esteem.
Dr Richard Winter

There are products in the shops in my town to make us thinner, fatter, fitter; to make our hair darker, lighter, stronger, curlier, less grey; to make our cheeks redder, nails longer, legs smoother. Products to hide skin blemishes, get rid of wrinkles and reduce cellulite. Shoes that make us seem taller. Clothes to make us look slimmer. Whatever bit of ourselves we dislike or want to change, someone will have a product for us.

This cannot but increase our dislike of ourselves. 'I'm not good enough as I am.' 'Without this, or that, I will not be acceptable.' 'I must keep up to date.' 'I must do what the rest of the crowd do.' 'I must hide my real self.' 'I must keep up appearances.'

These products are not wrong in themselves. There is nothing wrong in having clean and shining hair, and perfume that lifts the spirits (provided that no animal has suffered in its manufacture).

But it is something of a condemnation that in Western societies there is often more spent on cosmetics in a year than is spent on overseas aid.

> 'What would you like to change about yourself?'
> 'Oh, hair, eyes, nose shape, lips, skin colour—oh, everything.'
> **Interviewer and female interviewee on BBC Television**

◆ Am I really only acceptable at the party with make-up on or with smart, new, trendy clothes?

◆ Am I being taken in if I believe that I am only 'cool' if I wear a certain colour this year, if I prefer a particular kind of drink, if I drive the latest model of car, if I go on holiday in the 'right' places?

◆ Is my life really better because I have an electric carving knife/power drill/double glazing/liquidizer/stereo/the right kind of jeans? Or is it that I feel it will make me more of a person? More as if I belong? More acceptable?

We pick up messages from our society that tell us we are not good enough.

Some of us pick up similar things from our childhood. Teachers, parents, brothers and sisters, tell us we are no good. We do not reach their standard. We are ugly. Unwanted. Stupid.

This is the sort of thing that we grow to believe about ourselves. It results in us having a low self-esteem. We do not really love ourselves. It is the stuff of depression and we need to look more closely at this.

25

Boosting our self-esteem
I'm constantly surprised at the extraordinarily beneficial effect that meditation has.

John Cleese

In my late teenage years, when the truth that life can be terrible was gradually dawning, I started trying to find out about Christianity. Life was unbearable without any religion. Would it be any better with it?

I went to one of those very 'hearty' churches. Do you know what I mean? Going to them is like eating that very knobbly kind of muesli that health food shops sell. As you gnaw and chew your way through it, it is such hard work that it is only the thought that it must be doing you some good that keeps you going.

This church was like that. I knew it was doing me some good—if only that there were such kind and friendly people there—but it was really hard work to swallow.

It particularly seemed to specialize in what I called the 'worm stuff'. The minister was particularly fond of telling us that we should all believe that 'I am a worm and no man.'

Utterly evil?

On quizzing the minister one day I discovered that being a 'worm' was about being sinful. Hmm. That made it as clear as a bottle of mud. Further enlightenment came one day when he talked to the youth club about 'total depravity'. We are, he told us, naturally and utterly evil.

Well, after about a year of this mind-boggling stuff I could make some sense of it. Having picked up clear messages that I was unwanted, unloved, useless, in the way, ugly and a pain in the neck since the cradle, this 'worm stuff' all fitted in very neatly.

The sense that I was making of the world was that I had got it right. I was evil, wicked, guilty, and unloved. The 'religious' message made my depression worse!

Many depressed people can trace their feelings of utter

worthlessness back to these kinds of messages that are picked up as children and young adults.

In most of my [school] lessons I felt worthless and stupid.
Sue Townsend, author

At eighteen I thought I had sussed life. But whatever I did, I was always left with a sense of utter hopelessness. The feelings of depression were clearly all that I deserved. I learned to say, 'God be merciful to me, a sinner,' but I never got any further. I sifted everything that I saw in the world through my 'worm-stuff sieve'.

Probably the minister at the hearty church did say other more hopeful things. But I never received them.

Say something righteous and hopeful for a change.
Oddball in the film Kelly's Heroes

I see now that my school teachers, who I was so fond of, were trying to tell me different things. But I sieved out all the things that didn't fit with my view that I was a hopeless and useless person. It took many years for the worm-sieve to stop operating. (I think it sometimes still operates even now.) I could only receive messages of my own worthlessness.

There are many things that can make someone think that they are of little value:

Parents being too busy

Position in the family. 'As the oldest I always got the blame,' 'As the youngest I could never do what the others could.'

Abuse, both physical and emotional, from a family member or close friend

Unsettled childhood—constant moving or no close relationships

Anything interpreted as rejection—'I wasn't worth loving.'

Absence of praise and affirmation in childhood.

Changing my self-esteem

Changing how we view ourselves is difficult! Extremely difficult. The first step is recognizing the problem—many people who are depressed do not realize they have a low opinion of themselves, and the power that the thinking has in their lives. Once we recognize the way we view ourselves (and that's not easy) we are on the way.

The problem then is that if I think that I'm a hopeless, useless, ugly, unwanted person, I am on one side of the rock face. Books by earnest psychologists and psychiatrists tell us that if only we were over on the other side (by believing in ourselves, making the most of ourselves, accepting our great value and so on) we would feel better and our depression would go away.

Hmm.

I can remember reading David Burns' book *Feeling Good*, on a beautiful Mediterranean beach one year. It explains that I need to be over there on the other side of the rock face. It has stories of people realizing their need to change their view of themselves, changing it, then leaving Burns' consulting rooms free from their depression.

It all sounded a bit unlikely to me. It made me feel even more depressed. ('Other people can just walk away from their depression, but I can't because I'm such a hopeless person.')

What it didn't tell me was how I got from one side to the other.

▨ How could I change my view of myself?

I remember, as I read the David Burns book, feeling incredibly irritated and cross with the whole world. I never finished reading it!

It was as if I had struggled up the cliff face to a point where someone was now telling me that, in order to complete the rest of the climb, I needed to be the other side of a wide chasm. The other side is beyond reach. There is no bridge. There is no one who can help me across. There are no ropes. I just cling on to one side, knowing that I have to get across.

If I believe that I am hopeless and useless, how can I possibly change that? It's true! I am hopeless and useless. To believe otherwise is just wrong. How can anyone change what they have believed about themselves since they were born?

Hang on. Did I believe that I was hopeless and useless when I was born? Babies don't think like that, do they? Isn't it more like, 'I'm hungry. You have the milk. Come here and let's get on with it—now'?

You are a beautiful human person.

Pip Wilson, youth worker

 ## How do we change from one side to the other?

Someone recently gave me a very helpful way of seeing the ways we view ourselves. These are the three Ss. (The idea is from the work of Lawrence Crabb.) They are what we need to replace our old views of our worthlessness. We need to develop them in ourselves to get from one side of the rock face to the other. They are:

security

significance

self-worth.

Depression is about a lack of the three Ss. If I feel

insecure

insignificant

worthless

then depression is probably inevitable.

The three Ss are things to work on in creative ways—writing, gardening, making things for the house and so on. It is a slow and painful process. But in our creativity, and in relationships with others, we discover that we are of value, of enormous value. The only things that seemed to be able to penetrate the worm-sieve and the brick wall I had built around myself were people who loved me and were prepared to sit beside me and hold my hand.

◆ Advice is no good.

◆ Telling us to pull ourselves together is no good.

◆ All the activities in the world cannot replace a bit of tender loving care, some human warmth and a hug.

Activities can tell us how we are thinking wrongly. They can show us what we need to do. They can show us something of

119

the truth. They can mean that we encounter ourselves in fresh ways. But they can never take the place of love.

We can see love in the face of a little child, a kind gesture, the startling beauty of the Rocky Mountains and the smile of a neighbour who reaches out to us in an act of simple practical friendship.

Factors in my own climb out of depression were the care of someone who listened to me, the care of others who would pray with me, but also the care of a friend who sat beside me and held my hand. She would suggest that we do fun things, she made me meals and we laughed a lot. Looking back on it now, the most significant thing about what she did was just being my friend when I was finding the going tough.

With love one can live even without happiness.
Dostoyevsky

However much our Deeply Meaningful Something-or-others (the things we believe about our world and that tend to keep us depressed) have defined our world to us as a love-free zone, there *is* love out there. That's another of the Great Truths of life. Love does exist. We may not feel it this moment, but that is not evidence that it cannot be found.

Even when we have no human love, the fact is that God loves us. Without human love however, it is virtually impossible to believe that there is any kind of love. Mostly, it seems, God tells us about his love through other people or things. For me, being able to see that there was love out there took many years.

A thought transfixed me: For the first time in my life I saw the truth as it is set into song by so many poets, proclaimed as the final wisdom by so many thinkers. The truth—that love is the ultimate and highest goal to which man can aspire. Then I grasped the meaning of the greatest secret that human poetry and human thought and belief have to impart: the salvation of man is through love and in love.
Victor Frankl, Man's Search for Meaning

When we are at the foot of the cliff, we say 'Rubbish,' to all that. Transforming the view into realizing that we have significance and are a 'beautiful human person' may take years. Of course, I don't know exactly *how* we get from one side to the other! What I do know is that somehow I made that leap across.

I found I started to believe in myself. I found that my self-esteem had changed. I began to believe that I was valued and loved.

I've worked with young people full-time now for twenty years—usually with kids who are seen as 'delinquents' or 'tough'. The hard, tough image outside is a big front it seems to me—inside there is a sensitive delicate human being who is hurting.

Pip Wilson

Activity

⤳ 1 How far do the 3 'S's apply to the way that you see yourself?

⤳ 2 Go back to the charts in chapter 19. When you have done a few of these charts, you will start to see some of the ways that may be keeping you depressed. Here are some of the types of beliefs that you might find that you have:

I must do everything perfectly.

Everyone must make it clear that they approve of me all of the time.

I must prove myself to be a worthwhile person through the things I do.

Any criticism proves that I am no good at anything.

I am only a worthwhile person if it is clear to me that someone loves me.

The world must be a fair place, so this should not be happening to me.

It's changing this unrealistic type of thinking that will boost our self-esteem and help us to change from one set of beliefs about ourselves to another more positive one.

See the **'goodenough' principle** in chapter 9.

26

Understanding the 'losses' in our lives

I am free to change and grow.

David Augsburger

The experience of depression is almost always about some sort of loss. I don't mean losing an object, such as a precious piece of jewellery, although that is a devastating experience. I mean the loss of something that was part of us as a person.

You will know what I mean if you have ever been burgled. It's not what was taken so much as that someone was there in your house. They went through your cupboards—even into the box where you keep your very special things. They stood in your room. They defiled it in some way that is deeply personal and yet very difficult to explain. Maybe it is to do with the loss of privacy, of feeling secure, of feeling that we have a place that we have made our own and that expresses our personality.

That someone stood there, uninvited, is traumatic. That is the sort of loss we experience in depression.

One helpful thing that we can do if we want to climb up out of depression is to try to list these losses. I found that a very hard thing to do. But having made a list—over months—I found that their power began to diminish.

It shows again that once we can identify the sources of our depression, we can start to understand in order to overcome them.

My tears have been my food day and night.

The Psalmist

In his book *Feeling Free*, Archibald Hart outlines four senses of 'loss', and suggests that it is helpful to try to identify what is affecting us in order to understand it and come to terms with it.

122

◆ **Real loss.** This is a real and tangible loss of something physical:

The death of a loved one

Separation from someone you love

The loss of an object of great personal value such as a family heirloom, a treasured photograph or an address book or diary

Moving from a house you love.

◆ **Abstract loss.** This loss is not about actual objects, but more about our personal life:

Loss of love in a separation, or being jilted

Loss of self-esteem in heavy criticism

Loss of self-esteem and ambition in being rejected for promotion or in a substantial failure

Loss of being needed when children leave home and the nest is empty

Loss of routine, and perhaps meaning, after retirement.

In my experience, because these abstract losses are not immediately obvious, they can be incredibly powerful. We should make every effort to identify them. Once I had identified my lack of self-esteem I was able to do something about it. Unidentified, it was a drain on everything I did.

◆ **Imagined loss.** This type of loss is very powerful as it is difficult to identify. They are the losses we brood on in our mind, and are deeply embedded in our paranoid thoughts.

'There you are, I failed again, doesn't that just prove that I'm no good.'

'No one loves me.'

'Everyone is against me.'

'I will always fail.'

'Everyone would be better off if I were dead.'

'I'm stuck with life as it is and I can do nothing to change it.'

This type of thinking is at the heart of powerful psychological factors in depression. It is 'negative thinking' that we must learn to counteract by testing and checking. (Just because she didn't smile at me doesn't mean she hates me.) We start to grasp what these imagined losses are when we are prepared to listen to the pain. What is it telling me?

I found that imagined losses were dominating my mind. It was incredibly difficult to identify and counteract those thoughts, but learning to do so has been one of the main ways I have been able to hang on.

◆ **Threatened loss.** Hart's fourth category is the fear of the future—living with the worry about what may happen:

Death of a partner or a child

Loss of a job

Loss of your home, reputation, career, health and so on.

These potential losses can be much more powerful than the actual loss would be. If my partner dies when I am thirty, I might be more or less able to cope without him by the time I am thirty-five. But if, when I'm thirty, I live with the fear of his impending death, it will still be severely debilitating when I'm fifty and beyond though he may still be alive.

We need to look carefully at our worries to see if we could be free from the threat of loss that we are living under.

▨ Activity

⤳ Try to list your losses. Use the four headings in this chapter to help find as many of the losses as possible.

I've always been struck by the way so many patients, if they do well in therapy, develop an interest in the meaning and purpose of life.

Robin Skynner, psychiatrist

27

Understanding stresses

Over-much stress or un-managed stress can bring a lot of trouble, but we can't do without it altogether. Stress is vitalizing, necessary, often enjoyable and constructive; if we look at it straight, we can learn to come to terms with both its effects and its management.

Wanda Nash

It is probably fairly obvious that some things which happen to us during our climb through life are stressful. In turn this stress can lead to depression. It all gets too much, and so our bodies give in.

If you got married, moved to a new town, started a new job, tried to make new friends but desperately missed your old ones, took out a large loan to buy a new house, then found that your new job didn't suit you, it would be a bit surprising if you didn't feel overwhelmed.

One big event, such as a bereavement, can give us the creeping sensation of being cut off from everything, alone and afraid.

Something else may seem trivial, but worries us deeply. We dare not admit how much it gets to us. We feel ashamed and guilty. Some people call these things which cause us stress 'life events'.

Life events

There are various charts of 'life events' that list things which may cause us stress. The one that I have used is adapted from the chart by doctors Thomas Holmes and Richard Rahe of Washington Medical School.

It starts with the life events that will probably cause the most amount of stress. But remember that everyone is different. What one person may find insignificant, another person may perceive as traumatic.

The idea of the list is to show us that if we experience more than one major life event (the ones near the top of the list) in a year, distress of some kind is very likely to follow. Two from near the top in twelve months could lead to severe stress.

However, although some of the items nearer the bottom of the list look uncomplicated, under some circumstances they can be the last straw. Things were bad enough as it was, we were just coping, but the thought of having to get ready and face Christmas is just the end! We want to cancel this year. We feel the guilt starting. We feel embarrassed to explain our feelings.

The fact is that any kind of change at all can cause us to feel disorientated, even if we perceive the change as a good thing, such as a reconciliation, or a great holiday.

Any change can cause stress. In this list the ones the most likely to cause the most stress are near the top. Two events from the top half of the list within twelve months could spell trouble.

Death of partner

Divorce

Moving house

Separation from partner

Jail sentence

Death of a close family member

Illness or injury

Marriage

Loss of job

Reconciliation with partner

Retirement

Health problem of close family member

Pregnancy

Sex problems

Major change at work

Change of financial status

Death of a close friend

Change in type of work

Increase in marital arguments

Taking out a large mortgage

Changes in responsibilities at work

Child leaves home

In-law problems

Major achievement realized

Partner starts or stops work

Starting or leaving school or college

Change in living conditions

Change in personal habits

Difficulties with employer

Change in working hours

Change in where you live

Change in schools or college

Change in recreational habits

Change in church or socal activities

Small loan taken out

Change in sleeping habits

Change in family get-togethers

Change in eating habits

Holiday

Christmas

Minor violation of the law.

Individual reactions to things on the list will vary enormously. For example, if Christmas was always terrible when you were a child, when the first decorations go up (in August it seems sometimes), you get nagging anxiety in the pit of your stomach. If

Christmas was terrific in the past but now you are on your own, that same feeling of pain will be there. So Christmas might be nearer the top of some people's personal life events list than others'.

The point about the list is that it can alert us to the realities of life for us at the moment. Depression will not inevitably follow, but signs of distress will be there and need to be recognized, thought about, listened to, and adjustments made. (Planning more rest, for example.)

If your life has been stressful, you need to be realistic. You will recover from things much more quickly if you learn to be kind to yourself.

When I recognize that in the last few months I have had more than my fair share of life events, I can fight hard to stop the stress pulling me down into depression. It is when we don't see or admit to stress that we are in for trouble.

Equally to be avoided is the sense that, as you have had three major life events in the last year, you should be allowed to be depressed!

Things may be easier if you talk it through with your family: 'Look, I'm sorry that at times I'm unreasonable. Things have all been a bit much lately, and I'm struggling a bit. I'll try to cope with it.'

What isn't so good is the utterly selfish bad-tempered behaviour that expects the world to work around us and our problems. I know I have been like that at times! There is something about depression that does make us self-centred and self-protective (we need to survive). At times that is a good thing.

But there is a great difference between deciding some things about our own lives that we want to be different (such as our domestic or work role) and selfish behaviour that insists that we are the centre of the universe. We must struggle to see when we are like that, and to stop ourselves.

Think

~~→ Assess your own life events in the past year or two.

~~→ Some things not on the list may have affected you deeply.

~~→ Write down some things you can control and change, such as what you do, or think, or how you choose to react to things.

~→ Write down other things you cannot control and change, such as a death or a lost job. Some depression may arise because we are trying to change, or refusing to accept things that we have absolutely no control over.

Activity

An important skill in dealing with stress is to make lists of what needs to be done:

~→ Put things in order of priority—what I need to do today and what could wait until tomorrow.

~→ Set goals

~→ Do what you can today rather than worrying about all that needs to be done.

Lord, grant me the serenity to accept the things I cannot change, courage to change the things I can, and wisdom to know the difference

Reinhard Niebuhr, theologian

28

Fears
God weeps with us so that we may one day laugh with him.

Jürgen Moltmann, theologian

Carrying on 'normal' life is a big pressure for a depressed person. It is desperately embarassing to have to say that you cannot come tonight, or go to work this week, because you are depressed.

Often people simply do not understand.

Some of my more extrovert friends who are depressed think that this aspect is slightly easier for them. They derive their energy from being with others, so meeting people may actually make them feel better. For those of us who are more introverted (those who survive and thrive by having time on their own), social life is a continual torment.

I never really resolved how to deal with this during the very bad patches. I didn't want to have to talk to anyone except my immediate family all day (and I needed long breaks from them). I didn't want to go to the shop to get the milk and bread. I didn't want to go out to friends who had invited us round. I didn't want to go to work. I certainly didn't want to go anywhere where there was noise and I was surrrounded by people.

Naturally enough, my apparent unfriendliness and unsociability was misunderstood. This just is one of the many trials of being depressed and there really is very little that you can do about it. We can try to explain to good and sensitive friends, but we run a great risk if we open our mouths at all.

Coping with phobias

Trying to get over the sorts of phobias that often accompany depression is hard work. Often others lack understanding, and we may be able to see how totally irrational it is, which makes us feels we are 'being silly'. Our self-esteem takes quite a knock. If I can't cope with taking the baby in the buggy down to the supermarket, I must be going mad! What do I fear will happen if I go out of the door?

Here are some of the fears that complicate our lives:

certain places

crowds

heights or enclosed spaces

certain circumstances—being sick, coming face to face with a spider, or being in a room where people are eating

being abandoned and left alone

sex.

130

There are many more. The phobia can be about anything—from the baby's cot to cash dispensers.

▰▰ What is a phobia?

A phobia is an irrational fear. It's like having a panic attack, but it is always about a particular thing that we can identify. (Unlike a panic attack when often we do not consciously know what it is about.) The symptoms are the same—overwhelming feelings of terror, loss of control, nausea, trembling, dizziness, breathlessness, palpitations, sweaty palms, a need to go to the toilet and shakiness or weakness in the limbs.

> **Phobias cut across class, education and income and most fears—with the exception of animal phobias—tend to rear their head in young adult life. They strike women more than men and are more common among sensitive or highly intelligent individuals.**
> **From a leaflet supplied by Depression Alliance**

Fears of things such as spiders or snakes are common, but so are fears such as

agoraphobia (a fear of open spaces or public places)

claustrophobia (a fear of being closed in)

social phobias (fears to do with social contact).

People often experience more than one phobia at a time. It is, for example, possible to be both agoraphobic and claustrophobic.

▰▰ What causes the phobia?

Phobias vary so much that it is not easy to work out what starts them. They are possibly started by some sort of traumatic event, such as a house move, or childbirth, or by becoming depressed. Sometimes they are about things that happened in childhood.

What can I do?

1 Ask for help. Doctors and therapists seem to be able to deal quickly and effectively with phobias once they are told about them. We need not disguise them and say that we are 'anxious'. If we actually check twenty times that we shut the front door, or fear going on the train to the point where it makes us terrified, we would do well to pluck up the courage and say so. If we camouflage our phobia as 'anxiety', the tranquilisers given may not actually help the phobia.

2 Find out some more information. (See 'Resources' at the end of the book.)

3 Take courage from the fact that many people get over phobias completely.

4 Gradually learn to do the thing that you fear. I found as a young mother that I could just about cope with going out if I held onto the baby buggy. Without it I would panic, but with it I could gradually teach myself that I could get beyond the front door.

I still have to plan life a bit around my fears, but facing them head-on is more effective than feeling that they are insurmountable barriers.

Valuing ourselves

We may feel that we are going crazy because of our fears and our thoughts. However, I'm told that when we worry that we are going mad, it is a sign that we probaby aren't. The really seriously mad people are not aware of their craziness. This may be only a small comfort, but it is at least some comfort.

Fears, phobias, suicidal thoughts and irrational behaviour are all fairly usual during a time of depression. The fears will go away. One day we will feel significantly better. Nothing is gained, and a great deal is lost, by 'blaming' ourselves and focusing on our uselessness and stupidity. We are valuable human beings.

Activity

↝ Make a list of positive things you can say about yourself, or about the ways you are dealing with your fears and depression.

I'm trying to be kind to myself.

I'm going to get out of this depression one step at a time.

I'm good at my job.

I'm a 'goodenough' parent.

I've got some really great friends.

I'm working hard on the way I'm thinking and feeling . . . and I'm working at being patient!

I've got more realistic expectations of life now.

I've stopped giving myself unrealistic lists of things to do.

I recognize that crying is not being weak, but a way of letting myself say what I am feeling.

Sometimes even to live is an act of courage.

Seneca (first century AD)

PART 6:

FALLING OFF

29

Falling off

Suicide is a very permanent solution to what is usually a temporary problem.

Dr Richard Winter

For most of us, life is a constant trial. Falling off is a frequent occurrence. Things get so bad that we are back at the foot of the cliff again. All the old feelings come back. We feel defeated, crushed, and disappointed. We think through our options. Death is one of them.

Tempted to jump off

Most people think about suicide at some stage in their life. Some make attempts at it. The trouble with thinking about it even once is that the thought comes back. At the first sign of trouble our mind immediately flips into 'jumping off mode'. We become convinced that the world would be better without us. We don't think we can stand another minute.

Talking with friends who have had many suicidal thoughts, we all agree on is that it was our 'illness' telling us that we would rather be dead. When we get better, we are overwhelmed with remorse at our thoughts, and so unbelievably grateful that we did not harm ourselves that it is almost too much to think about it.

Many suicide attempts are angry responses to difficult relationships or situations.

Dr Richard Winter

Those around us, who we assume would be glad to get us out of the way, would in fact be affected for the rest of their lives by our death.

Taking all the tablets prescribed by the doctor in one go is dangerous. It may well result in death, but is more likely to end in irreparable brain damage. We wouldn't die. We would just become a cabbage.

Getting through the really unbearable patches

We need to be ready for these unbearable phases, when death seems quite a pleasant option. That's where our previously prepared collections of things for the really difficult times come in. This is in chapter 12. Different people need to do different things. One of the following suggestions may help you:

◆ Don't make any big decisions while you are depressed. You would make different decisions if you were better.

◆ We simply cannot know what death is like. It might be the end of all our struggling. But then again, it might not.

◆ Have a list of phone numbers of people you can ring. (In the UK the Samaritans are at the end of a phone twenty-four hours a day. They never judge. They will always listen.)

◆ If you don't feel you can ring people, go out somewhere. (I usually feel I'm unfit to be around people when it is really bad.) Do anything that will help time to pass so that the worst of the feeling evaporates a bit.

◆ Retreat to your 'cave'. Find somewhere where you can just 'be', where no one will disturb you.

◆ Although it feels like the bottom of the cliff again, it may be that we did not fall all the way down this time. What feels like the bottom may actually be a little further up each time. There is gradual progress.

◆ Cry, scream, write furiously, play very very loud music, kick the wall—anything that will channel the feelings of devastating and destructive depression into something other than the self-destruction of suicide.

◆ If it is the very early morning I find that I just get more depressed if I stay in bed. Getting up and making a cup of tea improves things a bit.

If in the end you are really determined to kill yourself there is not a lot anyone can do. But:

◆ If you die there will almost certainly be people who will say, 'I wish I had known how they felt. I would have liked to help.' You may feel that no one will say that. That is probably more a sign of the illness than of reality.

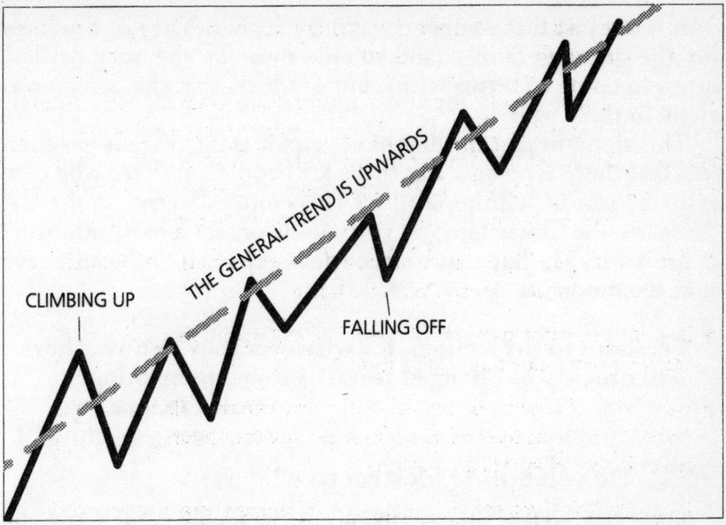
THE GENERAL TREND IS UPWARDS
CLIMBING UP
FALLING OFF

- **If you die, although you may not think so at the moment, some people would be desperately, desperately hurt. It would affect their lives for ever. (If that makes you think, 'Good, that will show them,' try to work out if you really want to give up your life for such vengeance.)**
- **If you die it may well not be quite what you expect. We can't know that anything would be better than our living hell. You run the risk of failing to kill yourself, but of permanently injuring yourself.**
- **Many suicidal feelings are a wish for some more help. What we are really saying is much more, 'I cannot stand this hell,' than, 'I want to be dead.' Tell anyone who will listen and will talk it through with you. Ideally tell your doctor. My doctor is brilliant. If yours isn't, change to a better one. It is very, very important to have a good doctor.**

The desperate sadness of suicide

When someone cannot cope with their depression any longer and their suicide is reported in the local paper, or in the magazine of Depression Alliance, *A Single Step*, I wish I could have held that person's hand until the worst passed. The sadness is overwhelming.

It is not just that someone was in such pain. Not just a sadness for the grieving family (and suicide must be the very hardest death to come to terms with), but a sadness that the person was alone in their pain.

This alone-ness at the depths of despair is the tragedy. We can feel that there is no one. But there are people out there who care and who can sit with us until we feel quite different. In the UK there are the Samaritans, or you could contact a local minister.

Sit it out. The hug that we need does exist—we just can't have it at the moment.

Trust not to thy feelings, for whatever they be now, they will quickly be changed towards some other thing.
Thomas à Kempis

Do something 'destructive'!

If this is making you angry—'How can she understand?'—maybe that could be good. Some suicidal feelings are anger turned inwards on ourselves. We become self-destructive. Recognizing and trying to express that internal anger is one step upwards.

It always makes me feel better to be 'destructive' towards something. Good choices, because the damage is only temporary, are lumps of clay in the garden, punching big cushions and so on. Bad choices, because we may regret what we have done but cannot alter it, are kicking the dog, breaking something precious or taking our own lives.

The issue here for our climb out of depression is that sometimes things need to be destroyed before they can be made better. The garden left undug will not give a good harvest. I once knocked down a wall in order to rebuild it. It was incredibly therapeutic—and from the rubble came a new and pretty good wall.

May the road rise up to meet you,
may the wind be always at your back,
may the sun shine warm on your face,
the rain fall softly on your fields;
and until we meet again,
may God hold you in the palm of his hand.
A Celtic blessing

PART 7

MAKING
PROGRESS

30

Picking ourselves up and having another go

The only way to heal the pain that will not heal itself is to forgive the person who hurt you. Forgiving heals your memory as you change your memory's vision. When you release the wrongdoer from the wrong, you cut a malignant tumour out of your inner life. You set a prisoner free, but you discover that the real prisoner was yourself.

Lewis Smedes

The good thing about re-starting, even if it is from rock-bottom, is that we know some of the possible ways up and some of the pitfalls. Not much else about re-starting is good! We know that ahead of us is a long hard climb. But we are not starting totally from scratch. It is a help that we know some of the handholds.

We learned last time that it helps to be kind to ourselves, to eat sensibly, to take exercise, to jot down the things that drive us crazy, to try to be a part of some self-help group, to keep adding to our store of strategies for the really bad days, and to do some of the things that we like doing.

We are now a little wiser. We know that it feels terrible. We know that some days are hell. We know not to take big decisions on the bad days.

Even those nearest to us (if we are lucky enough for there to be anyone close) are learning a bit about how to help us—or at least how not to make it any worse! (Remember that trying to help us is almost impossible.)

▨ Do I forgive myself—and others?

You will know no peace until you discover how to forgive yourself, to forgive other people and to let others forgive you.

Dorothy Rowe

Those who hang onto old hates and bitternesses, and who refuse to forgive or 'let go', are people who become hateful and bitter themselves. Those who are self-centred, bitter and angry are a pain in the neck to be with. Bitterness and resentment are ugly things. You can see them in people's faces.

In great contrast, the old person whose face is alive with forgiveness, love and the wisdom of old age is a delight and a pleasure to be with.

No matter what has happened—how traumatic, unjust, unfair it was—we will make the climb easier if we somehow unlock ourselves from it. We must put it down, or we will be dragged down.

▨ Forgive and forget?

It is not true that we must forgive and forget. Forgive, yes, but forgetting seems unrealistic, and at times impossible. Some things are so drastic that we are unlikely to forget them.

What 'forgive and forget' is trying to say, I think, is that we forgive by blotting something out and not holding it against someone any more. Forgiveness is a continuous thing, it doesn't happen once and for all.

As the years go by, the memory of wrongs people have done us usually gets fewer if we have forgiven them. And we shouldn't strive to remember. But forgiveness is also about remembering that it was that bad, and that we love the person so much that we still forgive them. Lew Smedes explores this point very helpfully in his book *Forgive and Forget*:

Forgetting, in fact, may be a dangerous way to escape the inner surgery of the heart that we call forgiving.

Saying 'sorry' and getting the immediate reply, 'That's all right—it's all over and forgotten,' is not necessarily the best thing. Forgiveness is so much more than that. The immediate response is the only thing that we can do with a small child. They need to be quite sure of our love and reassurance, and our acceptance of them even when they are awful. But the real act of forgiveness is far too important to be rushed at and said glibly.

Forgiving is difficult

It is one of the hardest things about the climb up out of depression.

It's hard to forgive someone if they are dead. It's hard to forgive if the hurt was the event of their death. That hurts so much that you persistently feel rejected and abandoned.

It's hard to forgive someone who isn't sorry, or someone who is unaware of what they have done. Maybe there were the best of intentions. But it hurt you. Parents and children know a lot about this. Most parents seem to make terrible mistakes with their children. Then children do it back as they grow up!

It's hard to forgive when it is a part of an organization, or a huge and anonymous system, that wronged us. Losing our job, or our home, comes into this category. The health service may do terrible damage to someone who is depressed. There is nothing—or at least I can't think of anything—that we can profitably do. But somehow we need, for our own health's sake, to let it go and forgive.

It is hard to imagine, when a war ends, what pain and trauma the whole situation has caused. Most of the young military personnel come home, but they will never be the same as they were before. The families who try to cope without a loved one who didn't make it home will still be hurting for a generation.

Those who have been prisoners in a war will try to escape from their nightmares. People try to live alone in cardboard boxes. Shattered countries try to feed their hungry children. Others try to survive alongside each other in families. In each of those lives there is the desperate need for forgiveness. It will not come easily. Life is tough. As Paul S. Fiddes says,

Forgiveness is ... a 'shattering experience' for the one who forgives as well as for the one who is forgiven. This is because forgiveness, unlike a mere pardon, seeks to win the offender back into relationship ... Forgiveness involves an acceptance which is costly.

142

How do I forgive someone?

Forgiving is difficult. Something wrong was done to me. It shouldn't have happened, but it did. Nothing can change the event.

What can change is the effect of the event on me. The person who did wrong should be brought to justice. But forgiving is me saying that I will not demand this justice. I will go beyond that. I will not stand on my rights—I will let it go.

Moving beyond ordinary human justice is the central core of forgiveness. When we are able to do that 'letting go', we say in effect that we are not going to let the past dictate the future.

Of course it is incredibly hard to forgive. But when I consider the way in which I believe God forgives and loves me, then I find I can think of forgiving others. Mostly!

Not forgiving makes life even harder

Not to forgive will eventually cause our fingers to stiffen as we persist in pointing accusingly at the one who caused us such grief. Pointing accusing fingers cannot grip the rock. We will lose our handhold and slip back two steps for every one that we take.

> **Vengeance is too little. Pardon is very much bigger and greater.**
>
> **Madame Irené Laure**

Our bodies will speak of bitterness and unresolved anger. We won't be climbing for any reason other than to get back at them—to prove them wrong. Not a good reason for climbing.

The burden of it will slow us down, and should we reach the top, it will have been such an excruciatingly dreadful climb that we will be disillusioned and shattered. The summit will hold no joy, only another reason to complain.

An act of the will

Forgiveness is something that we can choose to do even if we do not 'feel' able to do it perfectly. Forgiving is something that has a very definite start. That start is deciding that in the end we will forgive—even if at the moment we are:

◆ still angry

◆ unsure of what we feel or of what really happened

◆ feeling anything but forgiving!

Maybe there is such as thing as 'goodenough' forgiveness. It's such a long and difficult process that for most of us, most of the time, we live with things inside us that we still need to let go and try to forgive.

There are always people eager to tell us that we 'must forgive', while we are trying to work out what it is that we are feeling. As with many things, there is a time when it is right to forgive. We delay that time at great cost to our own wellbeing and our relationships with others.

Forgiving ourselves

Depressed people are usually bad at forgiving themselves. It is a common feeling that depression has come upon us because we are such terrible people that we deserve it. It is a just and right punishment. If you feel an unbearable amount of guilt, it may be that this is a sign that you are not forgiving yourself.

Putting down our burden of guilt

There is absolutely nothing that we can do that is too bad to be forgiven. There is no sexual sin, no wrong against someone that we love (or hate), absolutely nothing in the whole universe that cannot be forgiven and the burden taken off our backs. If we hear a little voice telling us otherwise, is it some voice that we picked up along the way?

Many people who become depressed wonder if they have committed 'the unforgivable sin'. They may not know what this means, but they remember the phrase from Sunday school. I used to worry about it but the best explanation of it, to me, is that it must be something to do with being so far against God, that you insist that evil is good. So, for example, someone may argue that torture is 'good'. They have turned against God so far that they cannot see it is wrong.

Almost certainly, our worries about it are unfounded. Someone helpfully said to me once that anyone who is worried about having committed that sin, is, by virtue of the fact that they are worrying about it, someone who hasn't committed it!

So if you are worrying about having done some unforgivable wrong, it's a sure sign you haven't!

If you are worried, ask a pastor from your local church for help.

Despair has been called the unforgivable sin—not presumably because God refuses to forgive it but because it despairs of the possibility of being forgiven.
Frederick Buechner

Guilt is perhaps the hardest burden to put down. It clings to us like a bad smell and has to be worked at until it has gone. It is far too heavy a burden for us to carry up the climb. When we are sorry (not an easy thing), when we have asked God for forgiveness, there is no place for guilt at all.

Even if humans can't or won't forgive us, or aren't there to forgive us, God can and does. When we are sorry, the wrong has been wiped out. We can hold up our heads now. There is a place for sorrow—but not for guilt.

If putting down the burden of guilt proves too difficult, get help. It isn't an easy thing to do. A friend or counsellor may be able to help us shift it off our shoulders.

The next stage

Once we feel free from guilt we can race off up the climb. But if you are like me you will probably find that, after a while, the burdens are right back there weighing us down. We seem to get curiously attached to them. During unguarded moments we seem to rush back to them and put them back on.

Life has for so long been depression, guilt, confusion and so on, that we find it difficult to realize what a life of freedom might be like!

Maybe the very idea of life at the top of the cliff, beyond depression, is frightening. If I'm not depressed people will expect me to cope, to be OK, to get on with life. Aargh! I'm not ready for that. Depression is useful to me. I can hide behind it.

We need time. Time to cope with the idea of what life could be like. Time to let the gaping wounds heal. Time to work through the yelling and the tears. The habits we have learned over a lifetime are not easily left behind.

> I have lost my daughter and we shall miss her. But I bear no ill will, I bear no grudge. Dirty sort of talk is not going to bring her back to life. Don't ask me please for a purpose. I don't have a purpose. I don't have an answer. But I know there has to be a plan. If I didn't think that I would commit suicide. It's part of a greater plan and God is good. And we shall meet again.
>
> Gordon Wilson, the father of a girl killed by a terrorist bomb at a Remembrance Day service in Enniskillen, Northern Ireland

31

Using our dreams to help us
We are not hypocrites in our dreams.
William Hazlitt

Dreams are another part of our lives that can help us to make progress. When this was first suggested to me during therapy, I thought it very silly. But I agreed to give it a try. To my surprise, it proved a valuable source of self-knowledge.

Dreams may be able to help us to find out what our Deeply Meaningful Something-or-others are—what is behind our depression, the cause of it. If we have pushed something down into our subconscious, tried to bury it instead of allowing ourselves to feel it, it may be that 'listening' to our dreams could help us.

Important things often happen to children when they are so young that they are not able to express what they feel. These feelings are still inside us as adults, creating havoc. Buried, they are like a bottled-up boiler in which the steam is building up to a dangerous level. The pressure is enormous and it might explode.

Our guard and defences work hard in our waking hours to prevent all that gunge and muck getting to the surface. When we are asleep they go off duty, so then it all tries to escape. It is trying to get messages to us.

◆ Please could you take some notice of me that when . . . died you were hurt?

◆ The reason you feel numb about . . . happening is you did not let yourself feel it.

◆ You were more deeply affected by . . . than you think.

Our bodies need us to *feel* that hurt, and to recognize what it is. Then we can start to deal with it.

These feelings, hurts, and unrecognized moments of pain are able to get through to us in our dreams sometimes. They may help us to add to our list of DMSs that are keeping us depressed. For some people, they are a way to self-knowledge.

I found a helpful book about dreams by Russ Parker. It was surprisingly easy to relate to my dreams on my own and to work out what my mind was trying to tell me. The really important thing that I found out was, as Russ Parker says, you must be ready to write down a few notes about your dreams immediately you wake. That's tedious, because it sometimes stops you going back to sleep, which is a lot to cope with if your depression is causing you to sleep badly anyway. However, as with so many things about the climb, this short-term pain can lead to long-term benefit.

The best way to get myself to jot down details of the dream was to:

◆ have the pencil and paper by the bed ready

◆ have a low-wattage bulb in my bedside light (a bright light gave me such a shock I instantly forgot the dream)

◆ write quickly

◆ never, never tell myself that I wouldn't need to write it down as I would remember it. If it is explosive stuff your consciousness wants to forget it. And it does.

Then in the morning I would read my notes through, try to remember the dream, add extra bits that came to mind, rewrite

147

bits that were illegible, and ask myself what it was that the dream was trying to tell me. You might find that this is something that you could share with a trusted friend, if you have one, but I found that I was able to get a surprising lot from it myself.

> **O Lord, you have searched me**
> **and you know me.**
> **You know when I sit and when I rise;**
> **you perceive my thoughts from afar.**
> **You discern my going out and my lying down;**
> **you are familiar with all my ways.**
> **Before a word is on my tongue**
> **you know it completely O Lord.**
> **You hem me in—behind and before;**
> **you have laid your hand upon me.**
>
> **The psalmist**

My dreams seemed to be a mixture of things that had recently happened, stuff so bizarre that I never knew what it could possibly be about, and old fears and nightmares that definitely rang bells once I got used to recognizing what they were about.

For example, one dream was about me going up into the attic of our house (I had been up there the previous day looking for something). I refused to come down. My therapist was at the bottom of the ladder telling me it was quite safe to come down, but I absolutely and vehemently refused, saying it wasn't. I wanted to stay up there among the spiders and cobwebs.

It was pretty clear what that was about. I was sticking to my old ground—depression and old thinking-patterns and behaviour—and refusing to let anyone help me. I didn't want to change or move down into the light. I was alarmed to realize it was true. I *thought* I wanted to change, but I didn't really. I felt safer how I was.

So dealing with dreams does come with a health warning. It is not easy. As with anything about depression, it can be painful.

Activity

~~➤ Put paper and pencil by your bed. (Make sure you have a hard enough surface to write on.)

~~> Change the bulb to a low-wattage one, or turn the light away from your eyes.

~~> Put some easy reading within reach if it helps you drift back to sleep after writing down your dream—(herbal tranquillizers too if you need them).

32

Loneliness

Loneliness causes greater suffering than cancer and leprosy.

Mother Teresa of Calcutta

Sooner or later each one of us feels utterly alone on this strange little planet. People tell us it is not so. We try to believe that it is not so. We belong to clubs and societies. We write letters to our friends. We make dates in our diaries to meet them. We put up photos of our family. But all this conceals the truth that hits us in depression. When it comes to the crunch, we feel alone in a world of millions.

Loneliness is more about how we feel than about the experience of actually being on our own. Almost everyone knows that awful sensation of being with people and, at the same time, experiencing devastating loneliness.

Psychotherapy may be available to us. We may have a dozen close friends, a wonderful partner. But in the end each person has to work out her own way of understanding the world. I have to learn to fight my own battles within myself. I must decide for myself which direction to go in—whether to get to the top of the climb, to stay here on this ledge, or drop off. No one can climb for me. If someone tries to live their own life through me (parents are good at trying to do this) it will drive me to distraction and then down into chaos and depression.

In solitude the lonely man is eaten up by himself.

Nietzsche

I am myself and only myself. No one hears the chaos, the ugliness of my mind or my silent cries for help. I'm there on the rock face, cold and alone. My fingers hurt. My arms and legs ache. My knees are trembling with the stress. I want to throw up.

This aloneness is the reality. Yet it is not the whole reality. It is only the reality of this moment. It is rather like the experience of winter. Spring will come, but it does not actually ease the gloom of the long dark days. The hope of spring does not warm us up if we cannot afford to buy fuel. It is all very well thinking of springtime ahead. Yes, it helps a bit, but the reality now is that it is dark and cold.

Life isn't just spring and new life. When we think of Jesus' death on the cross, the resurrection was not the whole story. The bit in the grave must have hurt him. He went through hell.

Loneliness is bred of a mind that has grown earthbound. For the spirit has its homeland, which is the realm of the meaning of things.

Antoine de Saint-Exupéry

Biology classes teach us that spring couldn't come without the death of the depths of winter. We realize that we wouldn't enjoy the first flowers so much if they were with us for the whole year. Maybe we need the death and the gloom to understand and enjoy the spring.

Without physical death, the resurrection of Jesus would be nothing more than a walk in a garden on spring morning. It would have no point. No power. To have resurrection you have to have had death. To know joy and peace, you have to have known turmoil and sorrow. Life without a struggle up the rock face would be a bland, boring walk in a flat boring countryside. Featureless.

So the aloneness is not the end of the reality. Maybe reality has a time dimension too and the end of the line will be both the suffering and the joy.

The beginning and the end of the line may make up one unit, but we only experience one bit at a time.

Maybe reality is made up of both the death and the resurrection. Winter and spring. It is both the isolation at my moment of crisis and also the comforting warmth of an understanding hug much later. (Sometimes it is very much later.)

Not having that loving hug at the moment of my pain is a problem of time, not a problem of the truth of its existence. It is not true that at the moment of pain that hug does not exist. It just doesn't exist now.

There is the lifeline, and the leader holding onto that lifeline. But I am at one end, and the leader at the other.

What is this loneliness?

There are many possible reasons why we feel so alone. Of all the symptoms of depression, the sense of being cut off and alone seems to be experienced by almost everyone. It is as much a part of depression as the feeling of extreme sadness.

As it is a symptom of our 'illness', we may come to see that the aloneness is not quite as clear cut and terrible as we sometimes perceive it.

Our being alone is as much to do with us cutting ourselves off from others as it is that others cut themselves off from us. People are there but we feel we do not deserve their friendship, or that we are boring people, or that they might reject us if we ask for companionship, or . . . Most of us have our own (often hardly understood) reasons for keeping ourselves to ourselves.

We may think we are doing the opposite of cutting ourselves off from people.

Ways out of the loneliness

If we have very few friends and relatives, to have any effect on a state of loneliness we need to make two basic changes:

◆ A change in how we are thinking about people so that we really believe (as opposed to think we believe) that we want to meet more people.

◆ Actually getting out and meeting more people. This probably means a change in how we behave.

151

Remember, though, that sometimes it really is that people are unfriendly.

How we think about people

Lonely people often have some negative self-talk (see chapter 18) that goes something like this.

'Well, I couldn't be friends with that type of person anyway.'

'If I make friends they will find out what I am like and then they will reject me.'

'No one would want to be my friend anyway.'

We are not so much alone, but experiencing the fear of what it would be like to be close to someone. Having friends and making relationships is a risky and painful business. We defend ourselves from it because we learned about how tough it was years ago.

Maybe we expect too much?

If we are unrealistic about what people are able to give us in terms of friendship and tender loving care, we will inevitably be disappointed.

A 'goodenough' friendship might be better than no friendship at all.

Activity

⤳ Spend the next few weeks arguing with your negative thinking about loneliness.

⤳ Get fit. Join a fitness club. You'll meet people, get healthier, look better and be more the sort of person people want to spend time with.

⤳ Join at least one other group or club. No one ever made more friends by watching television.

⤳ Make a list of people you already know. Plan who you could meet during this week.

- Make a list of the things that you like doing on your own. Feeling good about being alone is a part of the battle against loneliness.

- There are groups that exist for those who are lonely. Join a self-help group. Ask someone who runs a group for some addresses. See the resources list at the back of the book.

- Go out now and talk to either a neighbour or someone at the local shops. If you can't do that, write a letter or ring someone up.

If all your efforts come to nothing, it may not be you that is the problem, but it may be others.

33

Reaching the overhang and facing the impossible
The main thing in life is not to be afraid to be human.

Pablo Casals

The news on the television today is again too painful to watch. Wars go on, bitter and deadly. In Africa, soldiers take food that aid workers are trying to get to starving children. The television film shows tiny bodies being buried in shallow graves in the sand. Other children stand around, too weak to bother to brush the flies from their faces. A mother weeps, holding her starving baby to her empty breast.

My own child is confused at the death of one of her favourite teachers. How can I start to explain why someone so delightful and talented should die? What could I say to my children when their friend dies in a car crash?

How do we take them from the protection of childhood when we soothe them by saying 'it's OK', to the reality of life where it quite clearly isn't OK—at least not all the time and with no certainty that it will remain OK for very long?

We cannot explain our strange world, but no one could doubt the fact that it is cruel. Pain and sadness seem to come to everyone without any regard for how 'good' a person they are, or whether they 'deserve' to face such suffering.

Job, a character in the Bible, had problems like this. He was a good man but terrible things kept happening to him.

His 'comforters' tell him it is because he is a bad person. That goes down like a lead balloon, and Job tells them exactly what he thinks of them!

> **Miserable comforters are you all! Will your long-winded speeches never end?**
>
> **Job, during his depression**

When I watched a religious channel on American television, some preachers said that if we worship God and work hard we become rich and happy. That is one of the most ridiculous things I have ever heard. It could become a justification for letting the poor and homeless stay poor and homeless—because they didn't work hard like the rich did.

Bad things happen to good people

Any observation of human life soon reveals that awful things don't just happen to bad people. There are very rich criminals and poor honest people. Bad things happen to good people. Quite why God allows it I have no idea.

Saying that God has got it all in control, or that he moves in mysterious ways, is no answer. It may be true, but it's like people telling us we will be 'glad' we have been depressed. Really?

Maybe there just isn't an answer

Maybe life is such an anomaly that to try to give answers of any sort is doomed to failure. Maybe we will not get total freedom from our depression but develop an ability to handle life sufficiently well despite it. As time goes on, we get better at recognizing the truths about the pain of being alive.

The closest I ever get to finding some sort of satisfactory explanation of life and depression for myself is that we just cannot know the answers. Life has elements so inexplicable and so utterly awful that we simply cannot see what they are really about. It's like the smocking on a dress that I made for my beautiful god-daughter. The finished product, the stitches on the front, looked pretty, but if I looked at it from the reverse side as I was doing it, it was an incredible tangled mess of thread and knots.

Maybe in this life on earth we are always looking at things from this limited perspective—the wrong side. It looks a chaotic disorganized mess with no pattern or sense to it. But when we reach the after-life, we shall be looking at it all from the other side, and we will see the reasons, the pattern, the sense in it all.

Maybe!

Facing the impossible

Most people come up against impossible parts of life at some stage.

Some days we can barely cope with the overhangs, those impossible bits where we have to get over a huge lump of rock that juts out so far we need to go upside-down for a bit. Other days we are more able to deal with them.

Or we find another route.

Some days we look at what we need to face in life and it seems too difficult to face. Ever.

'Love her? After what happened?'

'Forgive him? After what he did to me?'

'Learn to accept myself! You must be joking!'

'Believe that this depression will end? Give me one shred of evidence that that is true!'

Getting over the impossible bits

◆ Work with someone on it. Join a self-help group. Ask your doctor for help or find a therapist. Never attempt an overhang without someone holding on very firmly indeed to the lifeline.

◆ Find a different route. There is usually more than one way of doing something.

◆ Don't make major decisions when the going is tough.

◆ If you can, choose the easiest option! Depression is quite bad enough without making things any more difficult than they already are.

There's no such thing as a peace of soul approach to religion. It makes of God a gigantic Bayer aspirin ... take God three times a day and you won't feel any pain.

John Powell

34

'You'll be glad this happened'?

In addition to trust in God, there will also emerge a trust in ourselves, a genuine belief in our own worth based not on endeavours but on the gift of being cherished ... we are acceptable to God because he is loving and merciful and not because we have done good things.

Myra Chave-Jones, Listening to your Feelings

Irritating people, who tell you that in the end you will be glad that all this hell of depression happened, just do not know what it is really like—or have forgotten. No one could ever be glad that it happened. But what does seem to be true is that having the low times helps you to appreciate the highs.

I'm not an authority on standing at the top of the cliff and feeling great. But I can see that in comparison with the bottom of the abyss, it is rather good.

Maybe if life was that good all the time we would become rather like brattish children who are so used to getting their own way that they become intolerable.

Perhaps the experience of being depressed makes us into 'better' people. By that I mean people who are sensitive and caring about the needs of others, and who have experienced enough about life to begin to develop some understanding of what makes people so varied and interesting.

We learn a growing appreciation of the extent of human suffering. In my own very narrow experience of life, I think I notice that those people who have suffered are those who are broad enough to open their arms to comfort those who are in pain.

One of the few good things about depression is that, like all pain, it is saying something.

Myra Chave-Jones

I suppose in climbing, if it were really easy to get up every climb, there would be little point in doing it, and we would not have the unique feeling of success when we get to the top. The harder the climb the better it feels. Maybe in some way we are made into more complete human beings if our climb through life is tough.

I don't know. That could begin to sound quite horribly trite. All I know is that though the people who tell me I will be glad this happened are quite wrong, often at the end of a really difficult climb I will stand at the top, utterly exhausted, but experiencing a feeling that I feel at no other time. It is as if I will never feel anything is difficult in the rest of my life. If I can do that, I can do anything.

Now that I have faced depression, and got better from it (even though at times I slither back down into it), how can anything in life ever seem as difficult as that?

Even if I think of the very worst thing that could ever happen to me—the death of my partner or one of my children—could that really be any worse than that clammy, silent hell? Of course it might be, how can I know? But having endured and overcome depression, I think that I have some of the resources to face the very worst that life might throw at me. I think.

Maybe it is those skills that I learned so painfully throughout those times of depression that will be the same skills that I need to survive the next thirty years. Facing depression is one of the hardest bits of human existence. If we can do that, we can do anything!

Tips for dealing with the 'pull-your-socks-up brigade'

There are enormous numbers of people out there who belong to what I call the 'pull-your-socks-up brigade'. Most of them are impossible to miss as they tend to be fairly vocal, but others are more difficult to spot. They can be friendly and sympathetic at first, then when you least expect it, they launch off into telling you to 'pull yourself together'. (If only it was that easy.)

Here are some tips to deal with them.

Beware who you trust
You won't get anywhere without trusting someone, but great caution is needed. People need to show themselves to be trustworthy. (You wouldn't attempt a climb with ropes you didn't know were trustworthy.)

The I'm-far-worse-off-than-you people are extraordinarily difficult to deal with
The really important things to tell yourself are: that they have desperate needs too, but depression is never, ever about a competition to be worse than the next person; We could easily become one of these people! Beware!

Beware of those who say they have never been depressed
They deliver this complete with a cryptic paragraph about how there have been many events in their life that could have led to depression. This really is no more than a complex way of saying that they are worse off than you are and that because they did not get depressed, you shouldn't either, so pull yourself together.

These people are to your recovery and wellbeing what a major avalanche is to climbing. You need to avoid them, or shut down your emotions and placate them, then make a swift exit.

Try to:

◆ Walk away. This is best done by suddenly remembering that you have an appointment (with your journal), or saying, 'Well I really must get on,' 'Duty calls,' 'I'm glad we've had this little chat,' 'How nice to talk to you'. Whatever you do, keep talking. That is absolutely vital. Any drivel will do, but you must keep it up until you are out of earshot.

◆ If you can't get away, smile benignly. Shut down your emotions at the same time. Developing this mask is a basic survival skill for facing depression.

◆ Develop a non-committal 'Hmm'. You need to practise this in your bedroom until you get it right. It should say neither 'yes' nor 'no'. People will usually take it to mean what they want you to mean. So, they tell you to pull yourself together. You smile and go 'Hmm'. They think you mean, 'Well, how kind of you Ross, dear, I never thought of trying to pull myself together. I really will try harder. Silly me. You are a darling to be so kind and helpful.' But what you actually mean is, 'You insensitive idiot, I could tear you limb from limb, you'd better evaporate right now or you're history . . .'

◆ Suggest you have a cup of tea/coffee/a coke. Prattle.

◆ If prattling fails, or you just haven't got the strength to do it, deflect them onto talking about themselves. Deflection is easy with the 'I've had lots of reasons in my life to be depressed but I didn't let it get to me' types because, like most people, they like to talk about themselves. If that fails, resort to politics, sex or religion.

◆ If you feel strong enough, being a bit assertive can do wonders. I'm not exactly suggesting that attack is a good means of defence, but assertiveness is a good thing to try to develop anyway. You can silence the most intrepid member of the pull-your-socks-up brigade by telling them that many of the world's truly great people were depressed— it's all a part of the creative spirit and a sign of true genius (in our case yet to be recognized). You can also get someone onto how they would arrive at world peace in three easy stages. This can usually guarantee to deflect even the most intrepid person.

There are other people, who tell you that you will look back on all this in ten years time and be glad of it, who are well meaning. They may have trodden the shadow of the valley of death themselves. Take great care. The best tack is to get them to tell you about it. Just like elderly and experienced climbers, you can learn a lot from listening to people like this, about what it was that made them depressed, and how they climbed out of it. If they are helpful, write down why. Then use that as a basis for yourself to help someone else.

You may not feel you could ever help anyone. Life feels as if it will always be this bad. But it won't. One day someone will reach out their hand for you to help them. Helping others is the only way I was ever able to make sense of the hell of depression, because it is like dealing with bereavement. You have to experience it to have any idea of what it is like.

> **Even though I walk through the valley of the shadow of death,**
> **I will fear no evil, for you are with me.**
>
> **The psalmist**

35

Missing the foothold
Why have you forgotten me, God?

The psalmist

The climb up out of depression is neither smooth nor easy. Some days or weeks we feel good and know we are making progress. Then, sometimes for no clear reason, our grip on life loosens. Something we thought we could deal with suddenly bothers us. Sleep patterns are disturbed again, perhaps with the dreadful

160

early morning wakening that so many of us experience. We slip back into old eating habits. We slip back into old thinking habits. The nightmares are back.

Suddenly we feel unable to communicate with anyone.

This has been my experience of the last few weeks. I know it is depression beginning again. I have learned to recognize the early signs.

It is not drastic or debilitating. Just a lingering tiredness and those tell-tale symptoms—bursting into tears at the slightest problem, waking early, already defeated, and finding that things that I have previously enjoyed are boring. Nothing is fun any more. Yet I know it is not that bad—yet. What I want to try to do is to not let it get any worse . . . Can I do that?

Stopping it getting any worse

First, try to establish that your hold on the cliff face is secure enough. It's not very secure, but it's secure enough. What I mean by that is that you have enough strength to face the next ten minutes. The thought of getting through the day is ghastly. The thought of facing next week (and the start of term) is so dreadful that I get panic attacks. But it is enough to be able to face the next ten minutes.

I've made a list of the things I *must* do today and those that I *could* do today. (I've tried to make it an attainable list.) It will make me feel good as I check things off. I probably won't get them all done, but everything marked off makes me feel good and gives strength to my grip on the rock face. I'm holding on well enough. That's 'goodenough' for now.

Secondly, be very aware of what is happening. This gives me the feeling that I have control over my life. First of all that awareness is simply that it is happening. Learning to recognize our own early symptoms is a crucial skill to acquire. Mine may be very different from yours. Other symptoms that friends have told me about are:

wanting to drink more (of the alcoholic kind)

extreme impatience

not being able to concentrate

a lack of interest in anything.

161

It is a good idea to note down how you feel in your journal. This may give you insight into those early symptoms. We might be tempted to see ourselves as sitting alone at the foot of the cliff in total darkness bawling our eyes out. That may not be the true picture. It may be that we are hanging on. Just.

Being aware of hanging on

This awareness of ourselves will only come with practice. There are all sorts of circumstances that can influence us profoundly and tend to make us think that things are worse than they really are. I find these are often related to physical wellbeing. For example, I know that one aspect of my present sense of slithering down the cliff is because I have recently had a virus. Any illness, flu or the mildest of tummy bugs leaves me drained and depressed.

I am also aware that simply being physically tired makes me feel things are worse than they really are. Being unable to cope after a late night is pretty obvious.

It took me years to recognize that what I call 'creeping tiredness' accumulates over the months. Looking back on my child-rearing years this was probably at the root of a lot of the depression—simple tiredness. In my case, unrecognized simple tiredness. If you are like me, this general fatigue takes over life. I went around like a zombie. It is important to develop awareness of what is happening to us. It's your body. You need to take control over what you do to it and what is done to it.

OK, so it's today, and I know that I am low. I know why—well, some of the reasons why—and I don't want to sink any lower. What can I do about it?

How do I stop slithering down?

◆ Believe that I am still on the cliff face and not at the bottom.

◆ Believe that things will get better! That's not easy. Especially as in the process of getting better, most things get worse. It's like tidying things—the kitchen cupboards, our desk, or the room of a three year old. There is always a terrible, terrible phase to get through first.

◆ Take great care of myself. When my fingers are sore and I know that my grip on the rock face is not as good as it needs to be, drastic action

162

is required. There isn't too much time for British reserve or a laid-back belief that everything will take care of itself. It won't. Firm and decisive action is needed. It is our self-survival that is at stake.

◆ Get plenty of rest. This is vital.

◆ Have a good diet with vitamin supplements.

◆ Some exercise really helps. I feel invigorated, refreshed and renewed. Even just a few stretching exercises in the bedroom can help.

◆ Time on my own. An extrovert might take care of herself by going out with friends or having some people round to her house. That fills me with horror! The principle is to do something that we *choose* to do— without feeling guilty about it! Guilt, sitting around feeling sorry for ourselves, or expecting someone else to do something about our insecure grip on the cliff will only make it worse. There is no need to feel guilt at taking a break and doing what we want to do in order to get over some crisis. It's OK to have crises. It's human to have crises and it's OK to be human.

◆ Use the negative thoughts chart in chapter 18.

◆ Although I prefer to write, it is also important to talk to someone. There is a big difference between expecting someone else to do something about it all (in the sense of handing over responsibility), and the very sensible act of sharing our feelings with someone.

Recognizing the progress

Everyone has bad phases. Provided we can see that we are more or less safe on our bit of the cliff, by stopping for a bit and planning our next move very carefully, we will come to no harm.

Having a bad or a difficult phase is not the same as falling off:

◆ We're not at the bottom again

◆ We will learn something from this particular difficulty—even if it is only that we had forgotten how absolutely dreadful it feels to have a bad phase.

◆ We have a valid reason for pampering ourselves a little. (Great—an excuse to have chocolate.)

Think

⤳ Look back over the last few weeks or months and think about the progress you have made. There may not be much, but there is probably some.

Happiness is like coke—something you get as a by-product in the process of making something else.
Aldous Huxley

More about diet and exercise in chapter 14.

36

Reaching the top
Happiness does not lie in happiness, but in the achievement of it.

Dostoevsky

Everything ends. At least, everything that is on earth and within our experience ends. That is one thing that we can say is 'good' about depression. It comes to an end. For some of us that end is only temporary. For others the end is after years of struggle during which we become different people. For most of us, this 'end' is not a mountain top of ecstasy. And it is certainly not the beginning of wonderful life, joy and eternal bliss! If we expect life to be like that we will certainly be disappointed.

But one day a moment comes when it seems that the burden has lifted. The climb seems easier today. We have an unexplainable feeling of lightness and joy inside our innermost being. We realise that the depression has lifted.

Yes. Experience tells us that it may not stay lifted, but we are

164

thrilled to get a bit of respite and we learn to take a breather while we can. This is a time to remember to write in our journal. This is an experience we must record as the memory of it will be crucial to our future wellbeing. Should the climb become horrendous again (and it probably will), to be able to read about the time when we felt great will be one way to cope. A way to survive. Evidence that life will not always be that bad.

There are two problems with feeling we have reached the top of the cliff. One is the 'tiger in the cage' problem and the other is the 'optimist' problem.

The tiger in the cage

There are several versions of the story of the tiger in the cage. It is about becoming so used to life as a depressed person that we continue to behave as if we were depressed when we aren't—'learned helplessness', some people call it.

The story goes that a tiger is shut up in a cage for years. She paces up and down trying to break free. She paces up and down for so long that when finally the cage is removed she continues to do just that. She doesn't see the significance of the removal of the bars and goes on pacing in the way she has learned, unable to appreciate the freedom that is hers.

We can be like that. Life is such a struggle that we learn to behave in certain ways. We expect life to be a drag. We expect to get exhausted. We expect to cry. We expect the days to be long and grey. We have learned to behave as depressed people. So when the depression lifts, we cannot recognize it. We don't make the best use of our freedom and we go on behaving as if we were still trapped in the horrors of depression.

The optimist problem

The other side is that we can be so excited when our depression has gone that we fail to make allowance for the fact that it may come back. It's disastrous to think that because it has gone, it has gone for good. True, some people do get better from depression and it seems not to bother them again—at least not to return with such intensity. But the realistic thing to do is to be thrilled at reaching the top of the cliff, but be ready for the next bit of the climb.

At no time is life one long party without troubles and cares. It's like climbing Helvellyn in the English Lake District. You just get to what you think is the top and then you see another summit some way off.

On several occasions I have made the mistake of letting myself think that the depression is over for good. I get so carried away with how fantastic it feels to be free of it that I forget to be realistic. Then when the old depressed feelings return, they come as a terrible shock.

The most useful thing I have been taught about the good times is to use them as preparation for the bad times. Rather like the idea of putting out a safety net. Life does feel a bit like walking a tightrope. One slip and that's it—you're off. But if there is a safety net, we need not worry.

We may as well accept that we are going to fall off. So, while we are feeling OK, it is a good idea to prepare for those bad days. We make plans for what we will do when we fall off. The idea is to be able to:

◆ recall the good times—this will help us to see that the depression will come to an end

◆ prepare strategies for how to deal with the awfulness of depression

◆ learn more about ourselves. What is it that I like doing and that makes me feel good; what is it that makes me depressed?

◆ learn to be kind to ourselves.

These things will help so that when we do fall it is only a little loss of dignity, and we can bounce safely on the cliff face. When we can get our feet onto a ledge, we can prepare for the climb again.

Maybe it is better to imagine that the climb of life is one that goes on for ever. Sometimes we get to the top of this cliff and the way ahead is a mile of springy turf. But there is another cliff ahead.

For now though, the climb has ended. It is flat. The sun is shining, the puffins are flying in and out of their burrows, the sea-pinks are beautiful and the smell of the ocean is exhilarating. It feels like heaven.

We would be pessimists of the very worst kind if we let the thought of the climb ahead weigh us down so much that we lost the the delights of today. Yes, we must keep it in our minds—life will not always be this good—but we must let ourselves enjoy the sheer excitement of the freedom that today, at least, is good.

Joy is the infallible sign of the presence of God.
Madeleine L'Engle

Good days have become for me like the very end of the C.S. Lewis Narnia stories. At the end of *The Last Battle*, when the world of Narnia comes to an end and the high king Peter pulls shut the door on the dead world, the children follow Aslan and the animals into a world that is bigger, brighter and better than Narnia. Yet it too is Narnia. It is all that they have loved and more. Aslan urges them 'Further up and further in!' and the dogs, the children and the unicorn run further into their new heaven, each bit getting better than the bit before.

That's how it seems on the good days, and we try to go further on and further in. But there still may be huge cliffs ahead of us. Life, it would seem, is always a journey.

My greatest asset is that I am constantly changing.
Jane Fonda

The choice

Ultimately I have a choice. I can go on fighting reality and insisting that life 'should' be wonderful, carefree, happy and so on. The sort of world-owes-me-a-living attitude that some depressed people (and others) demonstrate.

Or I can get down to the nitty-gritty of it all and choose to take as my baseline that 'life is difficult'. This difficulty is about the complexities of ourselves and our long lifetime struggle to get to understand our inner selves. It is about the unpredictable and apparently totally unfair way that life (and death) goes on. Tomorrow my world may be shattered by the death of my child. If that happened, I know that I would just want to die too. I cannot know what is out there. That is how life is.

Given the uncertainties and complexities of life, maybe it is surprising that there is as much happiness in the world as there is.

> Happiness is like a sunbeam, which the least shadow
> intercepts.
>
> **Chinese proverb**

37

Now for the mountain!
Nothing is so beautiful as spring.

Gerald Manley Hopkins

The sheer joy of living is, inexplicably, here today and to feel it is great! The last bout of depression, six months of struggle, anxiety, fear and almost daily tearfulness have at long last evaporated. I realize that it may not last long. Today I intend to enjoy it.

I've been walking in my garden. The snowdrops are exquisite. The crocuses spring out of the lawn in daring yellow and the robins are building their nest in the apple tree. I wanted to drink up the dew and soak in the morning sunshine. It seemed I had never seen such colours, or smelt such freshness. It all felt new. Different. Alive.

The joy and pleasure that I feel today may be great because it is in such stark contrast to the last few months. The winter has been long and dreary. Some days were so bleak that it seemed as if life could never be any different. But maybe nature needs its winter, its time of rest and recreating.

Although I could never be 'glad' of depression, today I know that I recognize the joy and freedom because I've had so much of the trapped feelings. The pain that I felt helps me to recognize the happiness. As one of my climbing friends said to me, 'If we didn't have our lows we would never appreciate our highs.'

It's when it is all over that we can look back down the cliff and realize the help that we have had.

Maybe the view that we will be 'glad' that it happened comes from the understanding that there is something about suffering that helps a person to grow emotionally, to learn to understand themselves better, and consequently to understand others better.

Rethinking our lives

The growth towards accepting and understanding our depressed feelings, and seeing them in balance with all the other features of our lives, is a very personal journey.

As the spring comes we start to see new ways forward in life. The death and the bleakness are not the end. The seeds that we planted last autumn are dead, but in their place are new green shoots. That seems to be the way that our world operates. For new life there has to be a death. There has to be some stage of resting, of rethinking and replanning.

> **He who can traverse the pit of darkness will emerge a stronger, more compassionate person.**
>
> **Martin Israel**

Times of depression have been for me times to reappraise my life. Of course, I could not see it at the time. But looking back I can see how they were phases during which I was able to think about what I really wanted in my life.

I have come to see the depression as the start of seeing the reality. The world *is* a crazy and ambiguous place and a part of our journey is recognizing that and somehow learning to live with it.

When all is going well we do tend to take things for granted. When things are going badly, we become more balanced. We see what is really important in life. Money and possessions, career, status and other things society tries to tell us are of supreme importance come to mean less than the little things we can miss in our busyness. We become glad of the little things, like the smile of a child or the sound of the birds at dawn, or the joy at seeing the first flowers of spring.

> **Thou hast made us for thyself, and our soul is restless till it rests in thee.**
>
> **Augustine of Hippo**

169

There *will* be an end to our depression. We begin to see that end as we learn to see that we are valued as people. That we *are* loved, even although it may not feel as if we are.

All life itself represents a risk, and the more lovingly we live our lives the more risk we take.

M. Scott Peck

Depression can mean that life is much better than it was before. It is more honest. More based in reality. More about the things that really matter.

When we get to the top of the cliff in rock-climbing, the harder our struggle has been, the greater our sense of achievement, relief, and, at times, ecstasy. At last we can lie down, rest our aching arms and just let the sun beat down on us.

We lie there, maybe a little amazed at what we have done. If we look with honesty at our lives and what we have been through, maybe we need to give ourselves some credit for sticking at it and surviving this far! To get even part of the way through a depressive phase takes extraordinary courage. To get to the end of it is perhaps the greatest achievement of our lives.

It is good to look back at it all and take time to remember what it was like at the foot of the cliff. Incredibly we find sometimes that we can hardly remember the very worst bits. It is as if they were so terrible that they become blotted out of our memories—a kind of defence tactic that we develop. It's rather like the way we forget the pain of childbirth as we take the tiny little person into our arms for the first time. The immensity of the joy blots out the pain.

Going on

It is so important in the good times to go on, not to go back and recriminate. Most of us have horror stories about the ways that we were treated during depression. Somehow we have to let these go. Otherwise we will be constantly moaning about how hard the struggle to get up was, instead of enjoying the sunshine and the rest at the top.

We don't know what lies ahead, but we must keep moving on.

I said to the man who stood at the gate of the year, 'Give me a light that I may tread safely into the unknown,' and

he replied, 'Go out into the darkness and put your hand into the hand of God. That shall be to you better than light and safer than a known way.'

From God Knows by Minnie Louise Haskins, quoted by King George VI in his Christmas broadcast in 1939, during the first few months of the Second World War.

I had this quote about going out into the unknown in my mind from the very start of writing this book. Writing felt like going out into the unknown. It is obvious that to some extent I feel vulnerable writing about my experiences of depression. During the two years it has taken to write it I have had some times of quite deep depression. It was excruciating to be writing about such terrifying fear.

Yet it has also been a joy to write it. I believe that our lives are made richer by sharing our feelings and thoughts, painful though this sharing may be. It is only when we reach out and take a risk that we can connect with others. It is then that the love, peace and new life at the top of the cliff become possible.

Sharing is one of the key features of the climb. We come to see that being human is about being a part of a 'community'. It is about relating to others. The annihilating aloneness of depression begins to be healed as we allow others to draw close.

When I come out of a depressed phase I read the words of the Revelation to John at the end of the Bible. They make me cry because they remind me of funerals of people I loved. They remind me of death, but also of new beginnings. John says that God will wipe away every tear from our eyes and that there will be no mourning or crying or pain any more because God himself will be making everything new.

In the beautiful picture, God is sitting on his throne surrounded by a jewelled landscape which we, as his children, will inherit. The crystal water of the river of life comes from the throne and when we drink from this water, we will never be thirsty or want for anything again.

Whatever the images used, this tells me that I am loved, and that there will be an end to the struggles and the darkness one day.

I am loved therefore I am.

Don't look down

We learn not to look down when we climb. We don't need to see where we have been. It's terrifying anyway. We only need to remember to learn from it.

We must go on. The summit is our only goal. The handholds above us look completely inadequate, but other people found them enough, so we must have faith that they will be OK for us too. We need:

◆ to think ourselves into life at the top.

◆ to learn to trust more in the lifeline and those holding it.

◆ to have hope. Others, who felt just as bad as we do, did finally make it. We can too.

◆ to go on practising the new skills we learned during depression—being kind to ourselves and being in touch with what we are thinking and feeling.

◆ to keep on working at self-understanding and at building up our self-esteem.

◆ to learn to 'let go'. Hanging on to old hates and bitterness is one very effective way of slithering down again.

◆ to learn to accept that it is 'normal' to get fluctuating moods. It's 'normal' to have to go back a few stages before we can go on.

◆ to learn to keep on climbing. Life is tough, but the more we keep plodding on with the journey, the better we get at dealing with it.

Depression can be a new beginning. There *is* life after depression!

> Deep peace of the Running Wave to you.
> Deep peace of the Flowing Air to you.
> Deep peace of the Quiet Earth to you.
> Deep peace of the Shining Stars to you.
> Deep peace of the Son of Peace to you.
>
> **An old Celtic blessing**

Resources

Useful addresses

Here is a list of addresses of organizations that exist to provide help. You will not be a 'nuisance' if you write or ring.

If there is not an address here that seems to meet your need, look in your local phone book, or write to an address below and ask for information.

The Samaritans

Look in the telephone directory for your local branch. They will help, day or night. Branches all over the UK, in Australia, New Zealand and South Africa. (The Samaritans in the US is a different organization.)

> **Head office: The Samaritans, 10 The Grove, Slough SL1 1QP**
> **Telephone: 01753 532713**

Depression Alliance

This is a caring and friendly organization that provides support for the depressed or anxious. For a very small subscription you can join the growing number of self-help groups if you want to. There are really good information leaflets available and you are sent a newsletter which is encouraging, informative and great for keeping by the bed to dip into on bad days.

> **35 Westminster Bridge Road, London SE1 7JB**
> **Telephone: 020 7633 9929 (answerphone)**

MIND (National Association for Mental Health)

Information available about most things to do with mental health.

> **Granta House, 15–19 Broadway, Stratford, London E15 4BQ**
> **Telephone: 020 8519 2122**

National Institute of Mental Health (in USA)

Information about how to get help.

> **Division of Communications, 5600 Fishers Lane,**
> **Rockville, MD 20857**

Manic Depression Fellowship

8–10 High Street, Kingston-upon-Thames,
Surrey KT1 1EY

National Centre for the Treatment of Phobia, Anxiety and Depression (in USA)

1755 S Street, NW, Washington, DC 20009
Telephone 202 363 7792

Association of Christian Counsellors

173A Wokingham Road, Reading,
Berkshire RG6 1LT
Telephone 0118 9662207

For women

Mama (Meet a Mum Association)
Self-help groups for women suffering post-natal depression.

26 Avenue Road, South Norwood,
London SE25 4DX
Telephone 0181 771 5595

Women Helping Agoraphobics, Inc.

PO Box 4900, S. Framlington, MA 0170

Further reading

These are some books that I have found helpful:

Myra Chave-Jones, Coping with Depression, **Lion Publishing**

Myra Chave-Jones, Listening to your Feelings, **Lion Publishing**

Archibald Hart, Feeling Free, **Fleming H. Revel**

Thomas A. Harris, I'm OK—You're OK, **Pan Books**

Martha Maughon, Why Am I Crying?, **Zondervan**

Dorothy Rowe, Depression: the way out of your prison, **Routledge and Kegan Paul**

Dorothy Rowe, The Successful Self, **Fontana/Collins**

David Seamands, Healing Damaged Emotions, **SP Publications**

Lewis Smedes, Forgive and Forget, **Harper and Row**

Richard Winter, The Roots of Sorrow, **Marshall, Morgan and Scott**

Books with more activities

David D. Burns, Feeling Good: the new mood therapy, **New American Library**

Dorothy Rowe, Breaking the Bonds, **Fontana**

Russ Parker, Healing Dreams, **SPCK**

Midlife problems

Mary Batchelor, Forty Plus, **Lion Publishing**

What's the point of climbing up?

Norman Warren, What's the Point?, **Lion Publishing**

Help with meditation

Gerard W. Hughes, God of Surprises, Darton, Longman and Todd,

Joyce Huggett, The Smile of Love, **Hodder and Stoughton**

John Powell, Why Am I Afraid to Love?, **Fontana/Collins**

Ruth Connell, The Lord is My Shepherd, **Lion Publishing**

Desert Songs, Selections from the Psalms, **Lion Publishing**

Families

Robin Skynner and John Cleese, Families and how to survive them, **Octopus**

All Lion books are available from your local bookshop,
or can be ordered via our website or from Marston
Book Services. For a free catalogue, showing the
complete list of titles available, please contact:

Customer Services
Marston Book Services
PO Box 269
Abingdon
Oxon
OX14 4YN

Tel: 01235 465500
Fax: 01235 465555

Our website can be found at:
www.lion-publishing.co.uk